TRAVEL IN INDIA

OR

City, Shrine and Sea-Beac

TRAVEL IN INDIA

OR

City, Shrine and Sea-Beach

ANTIQUITIES, HEALTH RESORTS
AND PLACES OF INTEREST ON
THE BENGAL-NAGPUR RAILWAY

GYAN

Published by

GYAN

Gyan Publishing House
5, Ansari Road
Daryaganj, New Delhi-110002
Phone: 011-47034999, 9811692060
E-mail: books@gyanbooks.com

Distribution Network
gyanbooks.com
India, USA, Canada, UK, Australia

ISBN: 978-93-7169-607-4 (PB)

First Published, 1916

2nd Impression 2025

Printed at: Gyan Press, Delhi.

TRAVEL IN INDIA OR CITY, SHRINE AND SEA-BEACH

TRAVEL IN INDIA

RAMTEK : THE GOKUL DARWAZA AND TEMPLES.

TRAVEL IN INDIA

OR

City, Shrine and Sea-Beach

ANTIQUITIES, HEALTH
RESORTS AND PLACES
OF INTEREST ON THE

**BENGAL-NAGPUR
RAILWAY**

BOMBAY

THE TIMES PRESS

1916

CONTENTS.

A FOREWORD.

THE route of the Bengal Nagpur Railway Company, glanced at on the map by those who are searching for a means of visiting attractive points in India, may seem to lie apart from the show-places of the great Empire. This may be so in a measure. The line does not reach hill-stations such as Simla, Naini Tal, Mussoorie or Darjeeling, with their views of the snow-clad Himalayas—when the weather permits. Neither does it touch the cities made historical and of tragic memory by the Mutiny. But apart from these things the Bengal Nagpur Railway line possesses some of the chief attractions of India. It can in the first place lay claim to a variety of scenery that is in itself of unique interest. The route from Nagpur to Calcutta passes amid varying tracts of jungle and ghat and cultivated lands that produce a cinematographic variety of views such as is to be obtained nowhere else in India ; also the line passes many historical and beautiful places. None who has traversed this route under favourable circumstances of season and climate, such as are experienced in the cold weather, will ever forget for instance the prosperity and fertility and umbrageous beauties of the country that lies about

Raipur; of the trees in happy little copses; of the waving crops, now the brilliant new green of paddy, now the ripe golden yellow of wheat, now the nodding silver-grey of "bhoota." None will ever forget the glorious view of the fortress temple of Ramtek—twenty miles distant—lifted high above the green plain on a great hill, with the white towers of the "mundils" glittering against the blue sky like the snowy cap of a great mountain. Ramtek viewed from near or far is one of the things to be remembered as among the most striking the world has to give. Likewise all who have seen the great ghats about the Saranda tunnel, who have looked deep into the jungle glades, who have seen the last red rays of the sun light up some deep craggy precipice of a distant hill, will carry the memories far into distant years. The Chilka Lakes on the line to Madras on the other hand present a type of scenery unusual to India, but one of singular charm and simplicity.

For the historical interest there are numerous attractions. There are the repeated evidences of the greatness of Indian civilisations of the past; of the power of hands long since dust; of people whose names are now but a memory; of dynasties which have died so long ago that almost all evidence of their existence has been lost amid the mists of the ages. There are the hundreds of examples of the wonderful Orissan architecture at Puri and Bhubaneswar, the work of a forgotten civilisation and architecture, and, above all, the great ruined Sun Temple at Konarak; in these three places may be traced the rise of this type of building from its early ventures, through its culminating point, to its decline. There are the temple and fortress at Ramtek, example of the work of the Mahrattas, one of the greatest powers in India a hundred or so years ago; there are the temples of Simhachalam, to which one must mount by eleven hundred steps, of Sakhigopal, of Kalighat; and the old towns of Chanda, Ganjam, Vizianagram, all full of the memories of the past.

As regards health resorts, the Bengal Nagpur Railway sets store by the health-giving sea airs of Puri and Waltair, the only places within reach of Calcutta where one may enjoy the bracing wind of the sea, revel in the surf, and recall memories of a sea-side holiday at home. But there is also Ranchi, a delightful station high on a great plateau, and in the Central Provinces there are Chhindwara and Seoni, the healthiest places on the Satpura plateau and points where it is possible to recover from the effects of the heat of the plains.

Also, and this will perhaps appeal most to many minds, there are on the line unequalled opportunities for the sportsman, especially he who desires big game. Much of the line through the Central Provinces and also in Chota Nagpur passes through a jungle region in which wild game of all descriptions is numerous. Tiger, panther, bear, bison, sambhur, nilghai and chital abound in the Satpura ranges; in the region between Salekasa and Dongargarh; and in the wild territory between Jharsuguda and Goilkera. Tigers and panthers can be shot without a permit and at any season, but permission must be obtained and various regulations conformed to regarding the gentler beasts. For information upon these points reference should be made to the Commissioner or Deputy Commissioner of the various Divisions.

City, Shrine, & Sea-Beach

CHAPTER I.

The Queen of the East.

HOW much Calcutta means to India and the European domination in the Empire can never be conceived by those who are unfamiliar with the city and its universal importance; who know not the many matters in which she leads opinion in India; who are ignorant of her abounding trade and commerce; who have neglected to study their history upon the conquest of India, with special reference to the part Bengal played; and who have never visited her for sufficient time to realise why so much of India's prosperity depends upon the financial, commercial and traffic organisations of the city. Calcutta, in fact, although no more the capital, is undoubtedly the Indian City which not only attracts greater attention than any other in every way, but is regarded as the first British city of the East. Not only in commerce and finance does she lead; not only is she at the head of the richest hinterland of the Indian Empire; not only does she possesses more industries than any other town of the Orient; but she has a tender spot in an otherwise somewhat flinty heart for a few of the more congenial occupations and " hobbies " of life, and more picturesqueness than most visitors expect.

The rise of Calcutta during some two centuries and a quarter from an almost nameless settlement on the turbid and turbulent Hooghly to the proud position she holds to-day reads more like a romance than history.

In the August of 1690, Job Charnock, a factor of the East Indian Company, who had been in charge of their trade at Hooghly and at other points—ventures which were by no means successful owing to difficulties with the local rulers—was (after being expelled from Bengal) requested by the Nawab to return and found a new factory. The Nawab, in fact, had discovered the mistake he had made in driving away trade that not only provided him with much needed goods but also added considerably to his revenues. Charnock had long cast an eye upon the present site of Calcutta, then three trading villages occupied by Indians and Armenians. Also, at an early date, the Portuguese had shipped goods yearly from an anchorage in Diamond Harbour. Charnock's selection of Calcutta as a site for his new factory was, then, no happy accident. He placed his headquarters far nearer the sea than were those of the French at Chandernagore or the Dutch at Chinsurah, and he selected a point up to which the navigation of the Hooghly was not so difficult as in the higher reaches. He took up a position on the left

A RIVERSIDE SCENE, CALCUTTA.

CALCUTTA : THE HOOGHLY.

bank of the river—all the other European factories were on the right—and that gave him an advantage in dealing with the richer and more fertile places north of the Hooghly. Moreover, he was near the confluence of the Adi Ganga, the present Tolly's Nullah, and the Hooghly.

But all was by no means fair sailing. If Kipling was wrong when he wrote that an accidental "mid-day halt" of Charnock's expedition led to the selection of the village of Suttanutee as the site for a new fort, he is right when he makes Calcutta say, in "The Song of the Nations,"—

> . . . . . I am Asia! Power on Silt!
> Death in my hands but Gold.

For Calcutta was in the early days nothing but a death-trap. The banks of the Hooghly in the neighbourhood of Calcutta was then very much the same as the Sundarbuns to-day—nothing but swamp, jungle, and wild animals. The Maidan was a great stretch of malodorous marshland from which the monsoon winds blew foul miasmatic vapours across the settlement. The jungle grew close up to the houses. Tigers prowled in its depths and muggers infested its numerous streams. But death came chiefly from the diseases that in those days made the tropics the grave of the majority of the Europeans who came to them. In less than three years Charnock was dead as well as more than a hundred of his followers. A like fate awaited reinforcements, but still the English hung on, suffering agonies in the hot weather and the monsoon, lacking all the benefits that alone make life worth living to-day in the East, wanting even proper houses.

A BENGAL NAGPUR RAILWAY COAL FERRY ON THE HOOGHLY.

CALCUTTA: CHANDPAL GHAT.

For nearly seventy years the settlement grew and prospered in spite of quarrels with the Dutch and French higher up the river and far more serious disputes with the Nawabs of Bengal. Eventually, in 1756, the trouble with Suraj-ud-Daulah culminated in a seige of the city and of the old Fort William, in the flight of the Governor and many Europeans, in the slaughter of others in action, and in the tragedy of the Black Hole in which died 123 of the 146 prisoners thrust into the soldiers' cell in Fort William after its capture. It should be added, however, that the truth of accepted history on this point has been recently questioned.

Six months later Clive, the "avenger," and Admiral Watson brought a combined expedition up the river; Calcutta fell in three days, and once more the English were established in their city and fort.

From that date Calcutta has, despite the once notoriously bad climate, never looked back. Success has succeeded success; development produced development; increase begotten increase. Presently the East India Company made Bengal its Chief Province, Warren Hastings was appointed the first Governor, and Calcutta the capital. Then the city rose on the wave of progress which she has practically never yet left. The city is to-day the head-quarters of the jute and rice trade of India, the chief coal-exporting station of the Empire, the home of numerous jute mills and engineering shops; is renowned for the safety of its finance; is the head-quarters of three important railways; and is India's greatest miscellaneous port.

But it is not the wonderful evidences of an ever-growing trade—developing so fast as to have outpaced

CALCUTTA : THE BLACK HOLE MEMORIAL.

THE MAIDAN, CALCUTTA.

the preparations of the docks for both exports and imports—that will attract the visitor. Rather will he look for historical associations and centres; for indications of the struggles of past days; for noted buildings boasting a connection with the mighty ones of the past: for those remains of early struggles that cities won by the sword possess.

And he will not be disappointed. The centre of Calcutta—the very heart of the business quarter—alone bears ample evidence of the events of the past. Here marked in the pavement in front of the Post Office and the Custom House is the site of the Old Fort—that of the 1756 disaster, which Holwell and a few loyal stalwarts defended to the last gasp; in a side entrance to the Post Office the position of the Black Hole has been located and perpetuated by a marble tablet; at the north-western corner of Dalhousie Square rises, in marble, a replica of the memorial raised by Holwell to his hundred and twenty-three companions who died during the terrible night of June 20, 1756. The monument stands on the actual spot where the bodies were flung into an unfinished ravelin of the defences. The original memorial was removed under the impression that it gave offence in certain quarters, but Lord Curzon re-erected it at his own expense, wrote the inscription with his own hand, and caused the names of all who perished in the tragedy to be inscribed on the marble tablets. The monument is not beautiful, but it is one of the most pathetic that history knows. The tank in the Square hard by was the original Lall Diggie round which the Europeans of the settlement walked for their evening exercise in the eighteenth century.

CALCUTTA : GOVERNMENT HOUSE.

Parallel with Old Court House Street runs Mission Row with its Old Church and the residence in which died General Clavering, who attempted with Sir Philip Francis and Monson to limit the power of Hastings. Bow Bazar, which runs from the Holwell monument to Sealdah, was the route of Lord Clive's march back into Calcutta after his attempt to seize Suraj-ud-Daulah's guns in Omichand's garden (near Grey Street), but in which he failed owing to the descent of a thick fog. To the north is the ancient Radha Bazar and close at hand is Portuguese Church Street in which stands the Roman Catholic Cathedral, built in the eighteenth century. Recent excavations in Clive Street have proved the site of the old landing ghat. St. John's Church, the oldest building of its kind in Calcutta, contains a series of interesting epitaphs and memorials while its churchyard holds the remains of Job Charnock and his Brahmin wife, whom he rescued from the pyre upon which she had been condemned to suttee. Here also are the tombs of Begum Johnson, a wonderful old lady who outlived four husbands, and of Middy Billy Speke, whose leg was carried away (and who died of his wounds) at the operations by Admiral Watson when Chandernagore was captured in 1757.

In the suburbs there are additional historical spots, Belvedere, recently the official residence of the Lieutenant-Governor of Bengal, before the change of the capital, and now the temporary Home of the Victoria Memorial Exhibition, was built by Major Tolly, who gave a new name to the Adi-Ganga. But the interest in Belvedere lies principally in the fact that it was in this palatial residence that Warren Hastings held

HASTINGS HOUSE, CALCUTTA, BUILT AS A COUNTRY RESIDENCE FOR THE WIFE OF WARREN HASTINGS, NOW THE BENGALEE "ETON."

"BELVEDERE," CALCUTTA, USED BY WARREN HASTINGS AS AN OFFICIAL RESIDENCE.

his receptions as the first Governor ot Bengal. At the second gate on its western side, near a dark avenue, Hastings met Francis to fight the famous duel that ended in Francis being wounded in the thigh. The encounter took place near the Hospital for Native Troops, the entrance of which is in Sterndale Road, and Francis was afterwards carried to Belvedere, where he lay for three days before being taken to Calcutta. The little patch of grass in the triangle formed by Belvedere Road and the roads leading to the Old Alipore Bridge was formerly the site for many duels. So famous was the place for the purpose that the trees growing in the space were called the " Trees of Destruction." A stonesthrow away is the house in which Thackeray, the novelist, played while a child, and of which he drew a picture (at the age of six) with "the monkey looking out of the window, and old black Betty on the roof drying the towels." Hastings' House, in Judge's Court Road, a noble old residence standing back from the road, formerly used as a Guest House by the Government of India—the Amir of Afghanistan was once housed within its walls—is now to become the school house for the "Indian Eton," an institution for the sons of princely and wealthy families who wish their sons to be brought up in the European style. It was built by Hastings as a country residence for his wife. There is a ghost story attaching to the place—or rather two or three. For it is said that on moonlight nights—some say in the high sun of the afternoon—the inhabitants hear a carriage and pair of horses drive up to the door, hear the horses pawing the ground and snorting, and hear also the closing of a carriage door. They

CALCUTTA: THE CHARM OF THE BOTANICAL GARDENS.

go to see who has arrived and nothing is there! This ghostly narrative is attested on the highest authority. Hastings, by the way, lived in several houses and Messrs.

Burn and Co. have in their Hastings Street office the gold-edged crimson punkahs that formerly swung over the heads of the first Governor of Bengal and his guests at dinner. The house in which the first meeting of the Governor's Council under Hastings was held is in Bentinck Street and the upper room, which was the meeting place, is still preserved in excellent repair.

The old cemeteries in Park Street will repay a visit. Here lies the dust of the real makers of Calcutta, the men and women who gave their lives that an Empire might rise upon their bones. Many famous names still remain on the old tombs and it is noticeable that the majority of those buried died at an early age.

The most pathetic of many saddening records there to be read is that of the beautiful Rose Aylmer whom Walter Savage Landor loved and lost and whom he immortalised in the lines—

> Ah, what avails the sceptred race?
> Ah, what the form divine?
> What every virtue, every grace?
> Rose Aylmer, all were thine.
> Rose Aylmer, whom these wakeful eyes
> May weep, but never see,
> A night of memories and sighs
> I consecrate to thee.

Truly it has been said that Calcutta is "a great graveyard of memories." Here also is the tomb of Thackeray's father and of the soldier son of Charles Dickens.

The city has many beautiful streets and much striking architecture. To-day the tendency is to rebuild in a modern style adapted to Oriental needs and much of the business quarter is undergoing this transforma-

THE QUEEN OF THE EAST.

CALCUTTA : DALHOUSIE SQUARE AND THE POST OFFICE.

tion. But the older style of dwellings are more picturesque and in the European quarters many beautiful old houses tinted with yellow ochre exist in spacious and full-leaved compounds. Indeed there is no more striking combination of colour than that seen in Calcutta of stone-coloured walls, a brilliantly blue sky, and the fresh green of palm leaves. Among the other beauties of the city are the flowering trees, of which the gold mohur is especially prominent. In the month of April and May these great trees burgeon into their gorgeous blossom on all sides. The laburnum droops its golden showers in profusion and a wonderful purple creeper clings to gates and trees. The city is a pageant in green and flaming orange ; yellow and royal purple. In the cold weather the crimson poinsettias and a pink flowering trailing creeper keep up the tradition of the glorious colouring of the East.

But principal of all Calcutta's claims to the picturesque is the Maidan. Once a great swamp, this huge area has been turned into grass-land and provides the residents with a space for drill, riding, golf, football, cricket, tennis, walking, while the roads that cross it are popular for driving. Here and there avenues of trees add to the beauty of the scene. In one portion is one of the best kept race-courses of the world and there are also three polo grounds upon one of which the Championship of India competition takes place in the cold weather.

Trade and commerce are represented in the city by some magnificent shops, palatial offices, and above all, the docks and the river traffic. The Hooghly is always crowded with shipping of all classes—from

CALCUTTA : THE BURMESE PAGODA IN EDEN GARDENS.

the 9,000 ton liner to the smallest country boat. The heaving yellow flood bears upon its restless bosom the shipping of the world, for vessels of every country are continually loading and discharging in Calcutta. One of the principal features of the river traffic are the huge ferry boats in which the Bengal Nagpur Railway bring coal, still loaded in the wagons from the fields, from Shalimar to Kidderpore for export.

AN ADJUTANT AT THE ZOO.

Among the social amenities of Calcutta are attractive and well-patronised theatres and bioscope palaces. Now-a-days there is somewhere to go every night in the year—a vast improvement on the state of affairs only a year or so ago when practically all the houses of entertainment closed during the hot weather. There are also musical bodies which give successful concerts, occasional exhibitions of Indian Art, and a yearly photographic salon.

Exhibitions are represented by the Indian Museum, —a vast storehouse of unique treasures—the Victoria Memorial Exhibition, the Zoological Gardens at Alipore, which are becoming more popular every year, and the Botanical Gardens at Sibpur, a great stretch of land filled with rare and beautiful trees including the largest banyan tree known. It has been asserted by Bishop Heber that these gardens are the nearest approach that is possible, to the Garden of Eden before the Fall. The Eden Gardens, which form a part of the maidan are another popular resort in the evenings, when a band frequently plays.

One might go on writing of Calcutta and its glories, its attractiveness, and its appeal to all for many more pages than is possible, and this chapter can give only

CALCUTTA : IN THE BOTANICAL GARDENS.

a faint idea of the points of interest. Nothing has been said of the scenes in the northern quarter, which is a typical Indian city; of the Kalighat and Jain temples; of the many important clubs, residential social, and existing for amusement; of the sport of all kinds for which the city is famous throughout India; of the large number of churches and sects represented; of the Improvement Trust and its work; of a hundred and one other features. Calcutta to those who know the place will always be a city of happy memories, not only by reason of friends and associations, but because of its many natural beauties. Not the least of these appeals to the artistic eye are its sunsets over the Hooghly, lighting up the sky beyond the smoke of the mills in a gorgeous radiance; the maidan transformed into a world of black and silver under the great Indian moon; the feasts of colour in the streets where the golden mohur and the Bougainvillœa creeper bloom side by side. Calcutta, indeed, makes repeated calls upon the love of the picturesque that is implanted in every heart. Truly the city can, with justice, claim to be called "The Queen of the East."

CHAPTER II.

En Route to the West.

WITH Calcutta as its centre, the Bengal Nagpur Railway stretches out to connect the North of India with the South and Ceylon (*via* Madras on the M. S. M. Ry.), and the whole of Bengal with the coal mining districts of Bihar and Orissa, with the Central Provinces, and ultimately, with the help of the G. I. P. Ry., with Bombay and Home. In both cases the journey begins over the same route to Khargpur. There the line branches into three, going North to Adra and Gomoh and the coal mines *via* Midnapore of unhappy memory as regards sedition and dacoity; westwards to Sini Chakardharpore and "all stations" to Nagpur with several branches; and southwards to Cuttack, Khurda Road and Waltair. Adra is connected with Sini by a line which runs *via* Purulia, where a 2 ft. 6 in. gauge connects with charming Ranchi and Lohardaga.

The journey out of Calcutta is through typical Bengal scenery. Tanks by the hundred; palm trees and banana plants by the millions; jute and rice in the water-covered fields; mud huts, goats and pariah dogs are among the principal features of the landscape. The moist climate, the perpetual presence of water—most of the country is submerged for the greater part of the year—serves to keep the countryside green and pleasant looking, and Bengal is often almost beautiful.

IN AN INDIAN COALFIELD.

AN INDIAN COALFIELD: THE COOLIE LINES.

AN INDIAN COALFIELD: MODERN PLANT.

Seen in the glow of the setting sun or with the slanting rays of sunrise leaping over its myriad still waters, Bengal scenery will be long remembered. There is an atmosphere of peace, of prosperity, of quiet and busy happiness about the country. A luxuriant vegetation and ready fruitfulness are evident on all hands.

But Bengal is not wholly devoted to agriculture. After crossing the Roopnarain bridge, one of the chief engineering feats on the line, the train approaches Khargpur, which the Bengal Nagpur Railway Company have transformed into a great railway centre; a veritable hive of industry. Here are the headquarters of the Locomotive and Carriage and Wagon Departments of the Railway. The workshops were opened in 1904 and have been considerably extended since then to meet the ever increasing requirements of the Railway. Up-to-date plant is provided for the maintenance and building of rolling stock and the motive power is supplied by a central electric power house which also supplies energy for the lights and fans used in the settlement. The staff employed number nearly 7,500 including Europeans, Anglo-Indians and Indians. The area of the workshops is 150 acres of which 23 acres is roofed in. Adjacent to the workshops is the settlement where the staff quarters are situated. The settlement is well laid out on modern lines with a piped water supply and efficient sanitary arrangements. There is a commodious bazaar near the station, also a comfortable dak bungalow and pilgrim serai. The population is approximately 22,000.

Beyond Khargpur is Kalimati, the junction for the works of the Tata Iron and Steel Company in Bengal,

THE TATA IRON AND STEEL WORKS.

and the largest of the kind in India. There is an abundance of iron ore in the neighbourhood and it is now being worked regularly and hard. The plant consists of coke ovens with a capacity of over 500 tons daily, two blast furnaces producing about 500 tons of pig iron daily, four open hearth furnaces with a capacity of about 7,500 tons monthly and rolling mills to deal with the production of the steel works. The rolling mills produce joists, channels, angles and rails. The works were started at the latter end of 1911 and are now in full swing, about 9,000 people being employed. It is reported that steel for shells is being made here and in addition the Tata Works are now supplying many Indian requirements in the way of girders, bridges and other equipment.

Adra is the first station of importance beyond the confines of Bengal but, considerable railway centre as it is, it appeals but little to the tourist. Although its many lines present busy scenes in the spectacle of numerous produce trains in continuous movement it is too new to possess in itself any historic associations. Bhojudih and Bhaga, however, while of even more recent establishment, have a special value in the commercial world. For they are outstanding points in the great coal-field that stretches from this portion of the Bengal Nagpur line far to the northward. The collieries in this district are the wealthiest in India and it is they that supply Calcutta with its monopoly of the coal-selling and carrying trade.

The Bengal Nagpur Railway is here experiencing great developments. From Bhojudih a branch line runs out to Bhaga, the centre of the coal district, and from Bhaga a perfect net-work of lines—which is, moreover, continually being extended—spreads out to all points of the compass to touch the various pits.

The coal industry of India is yet in its infancy. And, mining being yet in the early stages of development, all modes of working are to be seen—the " kutcha " hand-worked system side by side with the most modern raising machinery, screening apparatus and loading plant. Here by the side of the railway, a long black siding humps high above the line with scores of dusty, begrimed ant-like coolies—men and women—loading with baskets on the head: a few miles further on is a patently new plant equipped with the latest headworks and a long row of mecha-

AN INDIAN COALFIELD : ANTIQUATED METHODS.

AN OLD-FASHIONED MINE.

nical loaders which pour their coal into the waiting trucks amid one vast full-throated rattling roar and a cloud of dust; a quarter of a mile off is one of the huge burrows diving into the womb of the earth which the nearness of the coal to the surface makes a profitable means of mining. Fifty yards down a steep slope yawns a cavernous maw, black as Erebus, which now emits a loaded trolley creaking up the steep incline upon an endless steel rope or swallows an "empty" with even greater despatch. In many directions great developments are taking place and new pitheads and pumping stations are rising with rapidity. Here the countryside has almost lost the appearance of a few miles back outside the coal area, where the tender green of the young rice waves in the wind and little clumps of trees offer a grateful shade; or where outcrops of volcanic rock and the lavalike sides of heaped conical hills jutting abruptly out of the plain suggest a gigantic upheaval during the birth of the world. The coal fields might almost earn the name of the Indian Black Country; almost, but not quite. For they are not all black with no green thing but a coarse-leaved creeper that clambers over dusty "pit mounds" as is the fate of that unlucky portion of Staffordshire that lies about the great coal and iron district north-west of Birmingham. But even about the Indian mines the herbage has lost its freshness, the dingy refuse heaps make eye-sores, and the line of dark sidings with their rows of black wagons loom darkly against the blue sky: yet the prospect of high stacks grouped with great wheels on high spidery struts suggests the majesty of modern industry and tells of the riches of the land.

THE SWINGING CEREMONY.

PREPARED FOR THE "SWINGING" FESTIVAL.

But coal-mining is not the only matter of interest in this district. For quite close to Bhojudih is a little station which boasts on occasions a revival of a ghastly and mysterious religious ceremony. At Santaldih, one station east of Bhojudih, the antique custom of "hook-swinging" is carried on. "Hook-swinging" consists of the hanging of men who have volunteered for the occasion to a long pole by hooks thrust through the skin of the back. They are then rotated at a height of thirty or forty feet for several minutes. The business sounds particularly ghastly, but its actual performance is not so revolting as would appear. The hooks are passed through the skin of the fleshy part o the back just below the shoulder blades. The operator, who is of the "lohar" or blacksmith caste and who enjoys the office and any emoluments that may accompany it by virtue of hereditary usage, stretches the skin of the victim to the utmost and seems to succeed in separating the epidermis from the flesh and muscles. At least, when the hooks are passed through there is little or no effusion of blood. The hooks, which are of the same class as those upon which meat is hung, are fairly blunt at their tips but they are

OORAONS OF MANBHOOM.

"FISHING," NEAR ADRA.

capped with a needle-pointed thimble which transfixes the skin with the application of but little force This instrument is transferred from one hook to the other as either is inserted and can be easily kept sufficiently sharp for its work. After the hooks have been inserted ropes are attached to their shanks and garlands of flowers are hung about the devotee's head and neck and placed in his waist-cloth, while a circlet of bells is fixed to each ankle. The "victim" is then conducted to the top of a ramshackle platform where he is bound to a stout pole, with his back against the

BRAHMINI BRIDGE: BETWEEN CHAKARDHARPORE AND JHARSUGUDA.

wood-work and with the rope attached only to the hooks and not passed about his body in any fashion. His whole weight is undoubtedly on the skin pierced by the hooks. At the other end of the pole is a cradle manned by sufficient men to bring the victim to an elevation of thirty or forty feet and he is then carried round laterally. In some cases the necessary movement is imparted by means of men hauling on a rope and running with it in the required direction. Sometimes in the early minutes of his ordeal a devotee eases the strain upon his epidermis by leaning his arms upon the pole, but he eventually allows the hooks to have their full pound of flesh. The "swinging" lasts from two to five minutes or even longer, during

THE ROOPNARA' BRIDGE.

which time he casts the petals of the flowers about his neck to the crowd below.

One sportsman, while undergoing this self-torture, has been known to play upon a primitive flute, and another, who possessed some of the instincts of the finicky aristocrat, shielded himself from the sun with an umbrella. On the devotee being released the man who inserted the hooks removes them and presses with great force between the two punctured holes of the wounds with his big toe, apparently to close them. The wounds are then dressed. In the evening a village dance takes place and the festival ends.

"Hook swinging" is, or has been, practised—for the Government discourages such barbarities as much as possible—over practically the whole of Bengal and Madras and also in other portions of India, and practically with the same rites. Many explanations are offered of its origin, but Mr. J. H. Powell, M.A., has left on record one of the most interesting in a paper read before the Folklore Society, which he illustrated with photographs, some of which are reproduced here. It is his opinion that the ceremony owes its existence to the system of human sacrifices which were practised in early ages and of which it is a commutation. He connects it with the extinct "Merish" sacrifice, n which the victim, bound to the proboscis of the effigy of an elephant, was cut to pieces by the crowd and the remains burnt. This was a fertilisation rite and in some cases the victim was dragged across the fields. The "swinging" or offering of the victim to all quarters of the compass Mr. Powell attributes to a derivation of former practices when unwillingness to make a human sacrifice was fighting with supposed necessity and humanity suggested the leading of one sacrifice to the half-dozen points at which six had before been offered, so satisfying the grimly pious readiness of the people to appease the desires of the gods and at the same time economising human life. He connects the practice with the need for fertilisation and the time of the year—the end of April or the beginning of May—for the adoption of the ceremony supports the theory. This is just before the monsoon season and the period suggests that the practice is one in common with many human sacrifices for rain in all parts of the world. Now-a-days the men to be swung have some definite desire in view; good crops, more children, or the preservation of those little ones at present alive.

THE ROOPNARAIN BRIDGE.

Frequent as the practice used to be, the efforts of the Government to discountenance a ghastly and useless spectacle have almost rendered "hook swinging" extinct. Now it is practised only in a few uncertain centres, and in some places the piercing of the flesh with hooks has disappeared, the person swung being merely strapped to the beam. But the "pious" and superstitious Hindu does not part with his religious observances easily, and many believe that with "hook swinging" forbidden their crops would wither and their wives become barren. Education, however, is doing much and this faint descendant of the awful horrors of human sacrifice is yearly losing its hold upon the people.

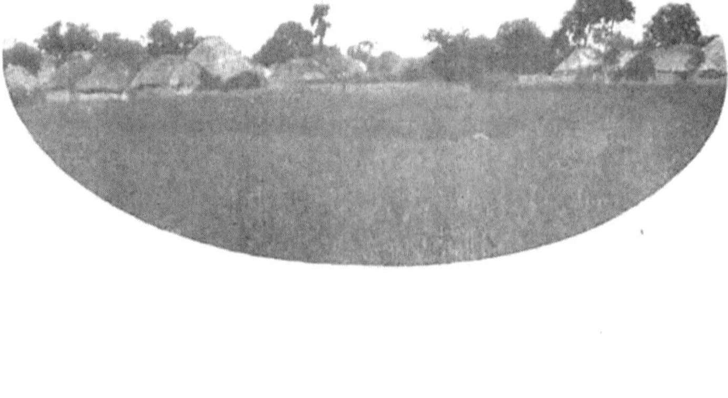

A VILLAGE NEAR ADRA.

CHAPTER III.

Saranda of the Seven Hundred Hills.

INDIAN railways have one distinctive feature; they run chiefly on embankments. One can travel thousands of miles on a track raised a few feet more or less above the level of the surrounding country until one forgets that there are such things as cuttings and tunnels. But, incidentally, it need not be imagined that because the railways seem to be of so straightforward a character that Indian railway engineering requires less ability than in other countries. Far from it, for if the engineer be generally spared the need for hill-climbing and burrowing and twisting he meets his difficulties in the numerous unreliable, turbulent, and even treacherous rivers that sweep through the country.

It is probable that no country can show finer feats of riverine engineering than India. The same river can differ so much in character as to be for all practical purposes two streams. In the dry season the river reminds one of the London lodginghouse tea, which, as most people know, has the unfortunate distinction of being so weak that it can barely summon strength to "crawl out of the pot." So the Indian river sometimes meanders along in a huge bed lying deep between precipitous friable banks and consisting either of heaped stretches and rounded humps of sand—glit-

SARANDA : THE GLOOM OF THE TUNNEL.

tering with mica and imprinted with the steps of thousands of feet, both man and animal — or else it trickles over great rocks, now flat like huge oyster shells, now jagged like the teeth of a saw. It lies in quiet pools beneath the shadows of boulders where the little frogs play hide and seek around the stones. It winds hither and thither tortuously with barely a ripple. Come the rains and the erstwhile stream is transformed into a roaring, seething, sweeping flood, yellow with the silt caught up in its mad flight ; bearing on its heaving bosom debris clutched from the hold of the infirm land ; filling its giant banks to the brim and often overflowing into the fields and villages. It is these mile-wide mad waters that the engineer in India has to bridle, to circumscribe, to render in-

SARANDA OF THE SEVEN HUNDRED HILLS: THE JUNGLE.

SARANDA : FROM ABOVE THE TUNNEL.

nocuous when he builds his long, high, many spanned bridges by anicuts, training works, and any and every means which his experienced skill suggests to be necessary if the waters are to be kept in subjection and the bridge is to stand against the assaults of the swollen floods of the monsoon.

But while the Bengal Nagpur Railway is generally an embankment railway it also has several "ghat sections" that necessitate the climbing of hills, much and intricate grading, and here and there a tunnel. The chief of these sections is perhaps that between Goilkera and Manharpur, with its lengthy tunnel at Saranda. At Goilkera you enter that picturesque district which has been poetically named "Saranda of the Seven Hundred Hills." And here you are in the heart of one of the most romantic districts of India; a land of mountain and living rock, of great forests and jungle glades, claimed to be the finest of the kind in India; of game even to the man-eating tiger—one of these gentry has a record of several years' activity and a reward of Rs. 700 attached to his evil head but so far he has proved too wily for the shikari.

These seven hundred hills form the watershed of the county between the Brahmini, which crosses the line near the pretty town of Panposh in majestic style, and the Subarnarika, which passes on its way to the Bay of Bengal near Sini and the Tata Iron and Steel Works at Sakchi. Their giant forests stretch from the south of the State of Keonghur on the south to the edge of the Ranchi plateau on the north and form some of the most important and productive forest lands of India. Close to the line the timber is plentiful even if it appears small, but inland miles of sal forest clothe the uplands, and the export of valuable timber is considerable. At many of the stations that stand in little clearings huge collections of trunks and giant mounds of sleepers can be seen. The scenery is always beautiful but especially so in the early part of the hot weather—the Indian Spring—when the hill forests put on their new dress of brilliant emerald green.

From Goilkera, where the ghats are entered, the line dips down into the heart of the forest amid leafy cuttings that seem as cool and shady as an English country lane. The line winds about in its endeavour to pierce a course amid the hills and at last round a sharp curve it plunges amid eerie scenery deep down in the quiet woods, into the Saranda tunnel, a passage bored through the living rock. Out of the clatter and dusk of the tunnel the train leaps again into the green shade of the forest—the contrast from the gloom of the rock

SARANDA TUNNEL : THE APPROACH.

to the sensation of living jungle is extraordinary—and then, just as suddenly, into an open space in the forest, full of warm sunlight. Here the forests recede a little from the line and one catches glimpses of the sides of steep grassy hills, of the dip and roll of wooded headlands, of emerald-fringed shoulders high above, of the whole mystery and wonder of the jungle, of a remnant of the world as it was in the beginning. It needs but to catch a glimpse of one of the shy people of the woodland—the dark Kohls with their scanty dress and fine physique—or of women bearing burdens slipping round the side of a hill; and to remember that amid these woods—so quiet, so serene, so peaceful in the sunlight—the tiger snarls at dusk over his kill, the sambhur dashes from persecution, the chital comes down to that shady stream to drink o' nights. the horned bison crashes his way amid the undergrowth, the bear shambles among the bushes, and the wild elephant changes his feeding grounds amid much disturbance, to realise something of the romance of this portion of the world; romance, moreover, that

CROSSING A RIVER.

is as near to Nature in its most beautiful as well as its wildest and grimmest forms, as it is possible to reach by any railway in the world and more especially one which has for its starting point the second city of the Empire.

From Saranda to Posoita the line winds and curves and rises and falls among these eternal hills; the train

SARANDA: LEAVING THE TUNNEL.

slips silently down grade, lumbers up with thunderous protests from the engine, and roars over high bridges crossing deep valleys. And every yard of the way the scenery has the same beauties and the eye is flattered by the verdant hues of the foliage, pleased by the incessant change of contour, held by the majesty and mystery of the aspect. It is with a pang of regret that one sees, for a time at least, the last of Saranda's seven hundred hills at Garpos but from Belpahar to Raigarh the train is again passing through jungles held to equal in beauty those of Goilkera, and you gladly accept these as an encore thoughtfully supplied by Nature.

CHAPTER IV.

Jungle Peak and Plain.

WESTWARDS from Jharsuguda the railway line enters the Central Provinces and immediately a new India—the great wild heart of the country, the India of tangled jungles and pug-marked drinking places; the India of wooded peaks and rocky cliffs; the India of dusty plains and roads; the India of big game in almost all its species; the India, in a word, of story-books. Here, as in many other parts of the great Empire, there are three distinct country-sides. There is the India of the monsoons, when the jungle, awakened to life by the crashing rains, leaps to maturity from ruin in a week; when the bare ground produces lush grass almost as one watches; when the trees put on their fullest dress and the undergrowth rises waist-high. There is the India of the cold weather, that beautiful season when the sun loses some of its power but the sky none of its blue; when the cool calm mornings and evenings make amends for the heat of the glaring day; when the land, fresh from the revivifying influence of the rains, smiles with gracious charm; when the crops whisper in the lightest breeze; when beast and man are well-fed and happy. And then there is the hot parched suffering India of the hot weather; of the terrible months from March to June, when the heat dries up the forest pools, and great rivers

A GROUP OF KOL WOMEN.

are reduced almost to a chain of lakes lost in the deep beds of sand and rock; when the green life and the goodness of the sap depart from all things; when the land gapes in fissures and the feet of beasts and men beat up the choking dust in clouds; when nature seems to have waved a wand of destruction above the naked groaning land. Of these three seasons the beginning of the cold weather shows India at its pleasantest and its loveliest, and the joy of travelling among a smiling country is that of the sojourner in those days when the sun of noon-day and the cold airs of the night are alike tempered and reasonable.

Before plunging into that land of deep jungles, fertile plains and plenteous hills one may diverge to the city of Sambalpur, south of Jharsuguda, by which the great Mahanadi sweeps down to the sea. In the monsoons the torrent is a mile wide, but when the waters have dried up, its volume has shrunk until it flows still more picturesquely among great boulders, sleeps in shady pools under the shadow of long rock faces, and reflects the flashing sparks of the dry sands. Here is

AN INDIAN TEMPLE.

historic ground, for Sambalpur was well within the scope of the raids of the Mahrattas—those warlike hosts of the Western ghauts who caused even the town of Calcutta, a thousand miles away, to build a great moat about the City to prevent a sudden sack by the tireless horsemen. The Mahrattas had an ancient feud with the Rajahs of Sambalpur, but those worthies scored when they captured guns intended for the Mahratta forts at Nagpur and which were being brought by water from Cuttack *via* the Mahanadi. That was in 1732, and the guns were mounted on the Fort in Sambalpur—a citadel of which only the moat and one gateway can now be traced. But the Mahrattas had their revenge, for sixty years later they stormed the fort after a five months' siege and re-captured their guns, levelled the great walls and bastions to the ground, and carried off the Raja and his son to Nagpur. Also Sambalpur had a reputation in Roman times, for it appears in the literature of that country as Ptolemy's Sarabac, and the Mahanadi as the Adamus River. In Ptolemy's map the Adamus flows into the Gangeticus Sinus, the classical name for the Bay of Bengal, and on its banks the ancients reported that diamonds abounded.

Fairly started from Jharsuguda on the stretch of nearly four hundred miles of rail to Nagpur the first place of interest is Raigarh, the residence of the feudatory Chief of the Raigarh State. Apart from a general picturesqueness, such as the snake-necked camel as a means of transport, the city is not greatly attractive, but at Champa, five stations further on, there is a temple to Mahadeo, a Hindu deity who is held to cure

BILASPUR STATION.

all diseases of the body instantaneously. The great festival of the year is held here at the time of Holi, the awakening of the country-side in the spring. Hence one passes on to Bilaspur, one of the chief railway centres in the Central Provinces, and the junction for the branch that runs through interesting country to Katni. Bilaspur itself is a thriving business centre and the aspect of the city from the station is an unusual one for India. The railway has brought it prosperity and to-day tussore silk, cotton, and iron-working present staple industries. Fifteen miles away is the holy city of Rattanpur, formerly the capital of the Hahai Bansi Rajputs, who ruled over India in 500 B.C. The town is in ruins but the crumbling walls of the old

A RIVER IN THE HOT WEATHER.

fort proclaim a former grandeur. The temple of Rattaneshwar is one of many, while there is also a sacred lake from which the greatest benefit is obtained by bathing at the time of the full moon.

From Bilaspur westwards for some distance the country-side is wholly devoted to fertility and the jungle has receded to the line of hills that dim the horizon. The flat fields run out from the railway as far as the eye can see and their new and brilliant green is an unusual sight after the darker foliage of the jungles. Here and there the wheat fields take on the familiar golden appearance of the English country-side at harvest time. Otherwise, too, the country is often reminiscent of Home, for here the typical Indian foliage of the palm and kindred trees has disappeared and the plains are dotted with timber of a shape and appearance at a distance very like to that of the great trees of old England. Very frequently, in this portion of the journey, one looks out upon a stretch of land that might well pass for a country six thousand miles away.

Raipur, a place of some importance and the chief town and headquarters of the Chhatisgarh division of the Central Provinces, lies in the centre of such scenery—almost indeed in an English park. Although Raipur goes back to centuries before the Normans invaded England it has little to show in the way of antiquities. Its chief attractions now lie in a fine main street, some two miles long, laid out by Colonel Agnew in 1830, in a fine maidan by which the town is approached, in a picturesqueness of population and a cleanliness of streets, and in the tanks and groves that surround

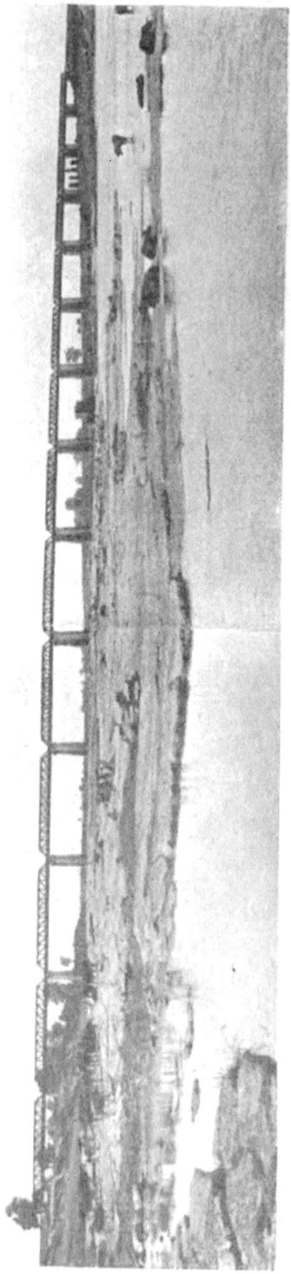

SHEONATH BRIDGE: BETWEEN BILASPUR AND DONGARGARH.

RAIPUR : PREPARING FOR A "DEWALI" DANCE.

the place. The great lily-covered tank which lies by the public gardens covers nearly a square mile in extent. An old Fort which was erected in the fifteenth century has now disappeared and there are no remains of the grandeur of Bamo Diva, the cadet of the Hahai Bansi house of Rattanpur who established himself and his court here in 750 A.D. Yet the old town has its charm. There is one long hilly bazar, which, from the quaint architecture and gaudy colouring of the houses and the bright raiment of the people—magenta and sky blue and orange intermingle with gorgeous effect—lives in the memory. If one happens to visit Raipur within a day or so of the Dewali festival, or "The Feast of Lights," one may see the Gowala caste making merry in an unusual way. Their celebration consists of a parade and

RAIPUR: THE TANK IN THE PUBLIC GARDENS.

much eccentric dancing in fancy dress. These gentry —the males only; their women kind being debarred from any such giddy exhibitions—attire themselves in the gaudiest and most unexpected of costumes. One will boast a waistcoat of damasked satin of the palest blue, set off by a soft collar once the property of a sahib and pinned with a gilt tie pin; long black stockings and plimsoles, and a gorgeous blue pugree to match his waistcoat. Another is made happy by an abundance of crude red and blue tassels about his breast; divers are proud of a collection of peacocks' feathers fastened behind the head and jutting over each shoulder, while a cluster of the same brilliant plumage is carried in the hand. As many as possible wear shoes and stockings—not their own originally but the cast-off effects of sahibs and even of memsahibs. A whole party will colour faces, arms and legs with "huldi," turning their features and extremities to a bilious yellow. Divers other bands appear in dhoties of one collection of shades, say from the deepest orange to the palest saffron. So adorned, the Gowalas parade the cities in knots of ten or a dozen, marching to the sound of a pipe—resembling in tone the high drone of the bag-pipe and lending itself to much the same class of music—and drums of all sizes. Many carry small brass shields and all possess "lathies" with which they gesticulate freely. The dance consists of a shuffle from one leg to the other and a turn; then of the accomplishment of a circle in single file and by means of a hopping step, while one enthusiast capers about, not at all ungracefully, in front, banging his stick on the ground, brandishing it in the air, and beating his shield. And anon, at a given signal, the whole party deliver loud shouts which might pass for "three cheers." Altogether the Gowalas enliven Raipur considerably after the Dewali, and the little town must be somewhat dull when these folk are diverting themselves only by adding to the milk the necessary amount of water to procure a handsome profit.

Southward from Raipur lies the town of Rajim, where the Jains worship in the sacred grave of Champa Ranaya, in which Buddha performed penance. The great mela here is in February and the fun lasts about a month. Forty-five miles from Raipur, on the same extension as Rajim is Dhamtari, a famous station for the Bastar and Nawagarh jungles, in which big game is plentiful.

Drug possesses a dismantled fort of great antiquity used by the Mahrattas during some of their depreda-

RAIPUR : THE GOWALA CASTE CELEBRATING THE DEWALI FESTIVAL.

tions, and Dongargarh has another reminder of the days when might was right in the shape of the remains of considerable fortifications. Here the line enters one of the best big game shooting districts in India; not only big game in the shape of deer (there are numerous herds of black buck about Dongargarh), but a more than sufficiency of tigers and other carnivora. Had there been one at the building of this section of the line with the descriptive powers of Colonel Patterson we might have had another equivalent of "The Man Eaters of Tsavo"; that tragic story of the ghastly depredations of lions during the construction of the Cape to Cairo route. For here, between Dongargarh and Gondia, the tigers of the Central Provinces seemed wholesale to have turned man-eaters while the Railway was building, and they have unhappily not yet lost their liking for human flesh. The tigers took the coolies from the camps at night, almost from the side of the fires lit for their protection; they pulled their prey off the ballast trucks as those vehicles bumped slowly over the uncompleted track; they became so familiar with the new activity in their hitherto unmolested fastnesses that they dashed out in the daytime and seized their "rations." Every effort was made by the engineers to destroy the huge vermin, but the brutes were wily as well as bloodthirsty and the tragedies continued until there was no need for hundreds of coolies and the temptation to strike down man—the slowest and least defended thing in the jungles—was partially removed. To this day, however, the district has its tigers and even its man-eaters. During one month a year or so ago thirteen natives were carried

DAREKASA : THE APPROACH TO THE TUNNEL.

off to an awful death. Two of the brutes responsible for their disappearance were accounted for by one of the Commissioners of the Division near the caves at Darekasa; the third is apparently still at large —unless "age with his stealing steps" has removed an unnecessary monster from the jungles.

The country side here, indeed, is for the most part "pucca tiger country." The line rises and dips and curves along an arm of the Ghats which carries thick jungle down to the very edge of the line; so close indeed that tigers can be seen from the train and "machans" erected within easy reach of the track. Near Dongargarh the jungle is somewhat open, and of bamboo and scrub, with great black outcrops of rock and in the distance the blue hills of a high range; between Darekasa and Salekasa the heart of a mighty forest is pierced by the line. On either hand stretch green glades with foliage so thick as to prevent the eye piercing ten yards; the brows of tree-fringed hills tower above the train; trees and hills stretch out in all directions—a wondrous pageant of the glories of the wild. And it may be noted that both east and west of these confines of the forest the mud houses of the ryots all possess a fence to provide some security from wild beasts, and at nightfall every home, every hut, every lodge at the level crossings, has its fire fed freely with logs to keep away the beasts by fear of the "Red Flower." Picturesque as are these flames on the quiet hillsides, each perhaps with the family group of gossipers about it, one is apt to forget the tragedies which have made them necessary.

North of the Darekasa Pass over the Ghats, near by which is the station of that name, a bold range of hills rises athwart the sky—a range partially wooded and partially of naked rock. In the face of the boulders that gleam red in the setting sun is a tunnel-like aperture. This is the entrance to the chief of a number of caves to which the wild Bhils of the district were wont to resort when persecuted. These havens were called "Kuchagarh" or "The Fort of Safety" and, guarded by thick bamboo jungle as they are, they doubtless well deserve the name. Near the pass the Kuardos stream dashes off the brow of a hill into a deep pool below and in its passage creates a picturesque waterfall. In the rains, when the water is pouring down from these hills to feed the plain streams below, this fall tosses up the spray to almost its own height.

At Salekasa, the next station, the outskirts of the jungle have been reached and from here onwards

BHANDARA ROAD : A NATURAL IRRIGATION TANK.

to Gondia some most charming pastoral scenery is to be seen. The woodlands still hold sway to a certain extent and extensive patches of timber group themselves about the country and about the pasture lands where numerous herds graze. Farther westward near Gondia the land is cultivated freely by means of a novel method of irrigation, and one unknown elsewhere in the Provinces. Tanks are numerous in Bengal, but in the dry heat of the Central Provinces they are as a general rule not in existence. The people of the Bhandara district, however, have overcome physical difficulties in the matter of the construction of tanks by ingeniously taking advantage of dips and hollows in an undulating country, much as a soldier uses "ground." Here a slight depression has been excavated until it forms a basin and the displaced earth heaped up at a weak point; there a long dam has been thrown out across sloping ground; in some places the lower hills of the ghats are brought into service; spurs are used as dykes, and chasms and fissures in the rocks as sluices. The scheme upon which this great system of lakes is planned is extraordinarily clever and indicates the existence of inventive minds. The tanks are by no means regular in size as in other parts of India but form rather meres and lakes. These artificial sheets of water number about 5,000 in all and one of them is seventeen miles in circumference and has an average depth of forty feet. As a general rule these irrigation lakes cannot be seen from the railway line except in a few cases, but now and again a great sheet of tree-fringed water glittering in the sun between Gondia and Bhandara affords some idea of

GONDIA : "CROSSING" THE CALCUTTA-BOMBAY MAILS.

KAMPTEE : THE KANHAN RIVER.

KAMPTEE : EARLY MORNING ON THE MAIDAN.

the extent of the lakes of this portion of Nagpur. The narrow gauge line to Nagbhir runs through country so watered. Bhandara town lies seven miles inland from the railway, and an overland connection between it and the Bengal Nagpur Railway's narrow gauge system to Nagbhir and Chanda is possible by road *via* Brahmapuri. The district is noted for fine silk and cotton cloth and a piece of thread so fine has been made at Chanda that a pound weight of it would cover 117 miles.

Gondia is principally remarkable for its activity as a railway centre. Here the mails from Calcutta to Bombay and *vice versa* cross and here too is the junction for the Satpura Railway, a narrow gauge which runs north to Jubbulpore in connection with the Chhindwara branch which traverses the Kipling Country of the "Jungle Book." Also there is a line which runs down to Chanda and connects at Nagbhir with a branch from Itwari.

Kamptee is a big cantonment town and apart from that point has little interest beyond affording picturesque views of the Kanhan river. However, there is a fair residential population of Europeans connected with the railways and various industries in the neighbourhood, and the fine shady maidan has golf links with muttee "greens"—if one may use the expression.

At Nagpur, the western section of the Bengal Nagpur Railway meets the G. I. P. Ry.,and Mails and passengers are handed over to the care of that organisation for the rest of the journey to Bombay. The distance to this point from Calcutta, *via* Sini and Khargpur is 703 miles. Nagpur has no outstanding history,

NAGPUR : ONE OF THE GATES.

THE TANKS AT NAGPUR.

NAGPUR : A QUAINT CORNER.

but was a prominent place in the past as the seat of Government of the Mahratta power established by Raghoji Bhonsla, the Kings of which line are buried in the southern section of the city. The evidences of this fame are not many but there are many picturesque scenes in the streets, the bazaars containing many beautifully carved wooden house fronts and pillars and here and there a gate in the Mahratta architecture that adds considerably to the Oriental appearance of the place. There is also a picturesque fort which overlooks the station, and two huge tanks. Industries are represented by two cotton mills which employ nearly four thousand hands and there are many attractive public buildings, including a library and schools as well as four public gardens.

Here then ends a stage of one of the most wonderful journeys of the world ; for a journey over any continent

KOLS MAKING A FIRE.

is wonderful and in India more so than usual. For here in the one country and under the one ruling power, have been found many varying scenes, many diverse types of people, many amazing stretches of country. From Calcutta westward the traveller has seen the flat swampy paddy fields of Bengal with their horizon of palm trees, sugarcane and jungle, and their lakhs of population give place to the jungle-clad heights about Goilkera and Saranda's " seven hundred hills " where cultivation is scarce and the only inhabitants a few of the least civilised of the people of India the aboriginal Khols who are still the children of the forest and take hardly to agricultural tasks and other regular labour. The forest-clad ghats have in their turn given way again to flat fertile plains where new crops have appeared ; where the bamboo open-wheeled shadeless bullock cart of Bengal has been replaced by a sort of woven boat upon heavy carved wheels, surmounted by a palm leaf cover and adorned on high days and holidays by a tapestried cloth ; where the people have dropped the white of Bengal for the blues and reds and orange tints that seem to perfect the Indian landscape. Then, again the country has slipped back to the jungle with all its dangers from wild beasts—the annual return of persons and cattle killed by animals and snakes in the Central Provinces is one of the greatest evidences of India's fight with the wild forces of nature. Once more the scene has changed to afford the spectacle of the fertility, the great trees and the pastoral beauties that make the smiling land between Gondia and Nagpur.

IN THE CENTRAL PROVINCES: A ROADSIDE SCENE.

The countryside is full of happy little pictures one would fain keep ever fresh in mind; would, if it were possible, fix upon a canvas to be often regarded. You remember for instance the great bulk of the heights about Saranda and the green slopes to which the ghats give way; many a boulder-heaped sand-choked jungle stream amid overhanging trees; slim dark herdboys —one of them with his sun-bleached curls and beauty of figure fit for an artist's conception of a godling of the woods—rounding up, with shouts and long sticks, the ruddy cattle and blue buffaloes of their village; gaily caparisoned bullocks, in coverings of blue with scarlet borders and a yellow cap inlet for the hump,

A VILLAGE IN THE CENTRAL PROVINCES.

trotting along with a gorgeously-canopied gari, filled with a wonderfully-dressed family party; little groups of ploughmen and their white cattle asleep under a tree during the slow hours of siesta; a dozen women in their sombre-bright dresses standing, sickle in hand thigh-deep among the waving wheat to watch the train rumble by; the sun rising in glory over a range of hills and leaping up with a sudden burst of golden light; the cool fresh air of evening when the last lemon glow gleams over the crest of the ghats and the evening star shines like a burning cresset above the woods; the sunset flaming through the trees upon an unexpected lake; the moon mirrored in the heart of a forest pool like a lamp; the cattle with their tinkling bells returning homeward when darkness is galloping up from the low ground and the smoke from evening fires lies in blue clouds across the woods; the fires lit for a protection against the wild brutes gleaming and glaring like stars in the darkness. You remember above all the cheerfulness of the people in their unremitting toil; the high thin cries of women washing at the pond; the songs of the coolies at their work. Last of all there is the stir of the breeze among the trees, the scent of the jungle and its flowers, and the hot dry dusty smell of the great plains at night. Here is India indeed and none can feel so far from Home as when these strange strong perfumes send their impressions to the brain.

CHAPTER V.

A Picturesque Branch.

FROM Bilaspur a branch line runs north-westward to Katni through a country which has many additional points of interest. It possesses, for instance some of the most beautiful of the sections on the line. The Pendra Ghats at the point where the line passes through them between Khongsara and Khodri are covered by dense forests, through which in the rains, thousand-feet-high mountain streams leap into the valleys, like threads of spun-silk or ropes of diamonds glittering in the sun. The view from Bhaor Tonk tunnel produces one of the finest spectacles on the line of the wild lands of India, while close by evidence of the legendary lore that forms a part of the life of the people is at hand in the banks of the river Amanala, which are planted with mangoes along the whole length of their course. The Indians attribute these trees to a miracle performed by a devotee. Sahdol, the modern town on the site of the ruined Biratpur of ancient India, possesses a tomb called Banjoga and the Temple of Kochika, a demon killed by Bhim, the champion of the Pandavas, in the great war of Mahabharat. The tree behind which the Pandavas concealed their weapons before taking their enemy by surprise is worshipped with much pomp during the Docora festival.

It is said that at Clapham Junction, one may book to anywhere in the world. Katni may be the

Clapham Junction of India, for it is chiefly remarkable as being one of the great railway junctions of the country, for here meet the Bengal Nagpur Railway, the East Indian Railway, and the Great Indian Peninsula Ry. From here the Bengal-Nagpur line passes down to Bengal, Madras, and Ceylon, the G. I. P. Ry. takes the route to Northern India and the Punjab, and eastward to Bombay. Also the Bengal-Nagpur Railway is opening *via* Katni, the shortest route from Calcutta to Karachi.

TEMPLE REFLECTIONS.

CHAPTER VI.

The Fortress-Temple of Ramtek.

> The splendour falls on castle walls
>   And snowy summits old in story.
> The long light shakes across the lakes,
>   And the wild cataract leaps in glory

ABOVE the fertile plain with its waving crops of "dewani" and paddy and its pleasant prospect of full-leaved trees leaps a ridge of well-wooded hills in a long hog-back range. Round their western extremity clusters a white-walled brown-roofed town in picturesque huddle. High above the little city, on the hill nearest the setting sun, the rocky hill-sides rise—from the distance—quite imperceptibly into the long frowning walls of a fortress. And above the stern rocks glitter in snow-white grandeur against the cloudless azure Indian sky a cluster of temples. Such is the Hill of Rama above Ramtek, one of the most famous of Hindu shrines and one of the most effectively placed. For the glittering temples of Ramtek, smiling above their frowning battlements, dominate whole districts as do few other great Hindu shrines, too many of which are hidden away among bustee or jungle.

Mythology and legend have been busy about this picturesque western peak of the Ambagarh range, and the hill, its temple and its tanks are places of impres-

RAMTEK : THE SACRED TANK MADE BY NARSINHA'S CUDGEL.

RAMTEK : THE BHAIRAVA DARWAZA.

sive sanctity and frequent pilgrimage for many reasons. In the first place the stone of this hill, when recently fractured, gleams like new bloodstains in the sunlight, and tradition has assigned this effect to the devilish blood of the demon Hiranya Kashipu, slain here by Vishnu in his Narsinha or Man-Lion incarnation. Vishnu, it is added, after his victory flung aside his colossal club with such force that it struck the side of the hill and dented the living rock deep enough to allow water to collect in a pool. Moreover Rama lived on the sacred hill and, indeed, lives here still, while in a little cup in the hills lies a sacred lake where miracles have been performed.

Let us follow in the footsteps of the pilgrims as they make their ascent to the shrine on the westernmost peak. Religious custom ordains that the pilgrims shall ascend to the temples by the great granite stairway that stretches up the easiest slope of the hill from the Ambala tank. This great sheet of water lying among the forest-clad hills, girt about with stone revetments, and reflecting a score of beautiful little shrines in its quiet waters, was, says the legend, the scene of a wonderful miracle in the forgotten past. Amba, the Sursavansi Rajput King, and a leper, while out hunting on the Ambagarh hills, reached a little spring deep in the heart of the forest. He descended from his horse to quench the royal thirst at the inviting place, and as he drank and laved his hands and face in Hindu fashion, he was amazed to see that the leprous disfigurement had disappeared from the parts of his body that the water had touched. For the spring at which he drank was the sacred Bhogavati

RAMTEK : THE AMBALA TANK FROM THE CITADEL RAMPARTS.

or the Ganges of the nether world ; as holy a stream as is Mother Ganga at Benares itself. And Amba, having proved the virtue of the water by cleansing his body of the disease, excavated the site of the tank and it filled with the holy waters. Now it serves the Hindu in these hills as the Ganges does him of the plains. It is even sacred enough to receive in its waters the bones of the dead.

From this peaceful place the pilgrims climb by a long and weary road to the temples on the hill. It seems that the builder of the road desired to make it as fatiguing as possible, probably as a physical preparation of the pilgrims for the mysteries of the hill above, for the Hill of Rama is also "Tapogiri", or the Hill of Penance. The steps are not steep and run in little flights and long "landings", but here and there, for no reason, they mount in three or four and then fall again by just as many to the previous level. Anon they are steep and anon shallow, but always they mount the tree-fringed, rock-sprinkled valley that leads to the gate of the fortress. Presently they cross the first line of the defences, now in ruins but in its prime a crenellated wall with square bastions pierced by huge loop holes. Here one may look back upon the pool of Ambala and see it lying amid its semicircle of hills glittering like a great jewel in the sun. Still the stone staircase winds upward, amid the ruins of a large village in the midst of which lies, emerald green among its old stone work and beneath a galleried terrace, the sacred waters that have occupied the hole made by Narsinha's cudgel when it fell after he had cast it from him on the slaying of the monster Hiranya Kashipu. Over against the tank is an old dharmsala or hostel and near by are temples of Narsinha with huge images. And here in a little bustee that fringes the climbing roadway, fakirs and pundits raise their monotonous voices in prayer, salaaming as they turn over a page, so earnest in their devotions that they pay no heed to the passer by.

Close at hand is the temple of Dhumreshwa Mahadeo—a "mundil" with a quaint traditional history. Here, it seems, one Shambuka, a Sudra by caste, lived in primeval times. He evidently had ambitions, for he

RAMTEK : THE SINGHPUR GATE.

practised austerities of far greater severity than religious observance permitted. This is why the hill is called the Hill of Penance. Curiously enough his piety resulted in the death of a Brahman's son, and Rama, angered at the tragedy, descended and struck off Shambuka's head. The Sudra, elevated in mind by the manner of his death at the hands of a god, prayed to Rama that he would abide for ever at Ramtek and that he too (the Sudra) might be worshipped there. Rama granted the request, and took up his abode on the hill, while the Sudra was turned into the lingam over which the temple of Dhumreshwa Mahadeo was built. As a sign, it is said, of the fulfilment of Rama's promise a flame, like unto the Morning Star, plays round the pointed iron rod above the temple. For the unbeliever it may be added that

RAMTEK : THE VARAH DARWAZA.

RAMTEK : THE BOAR INCARNATION OF VISHNU BENEATH WHICH PILGRIMS MUST CRAWL TO PROVE THEIR FREEDOM FROM SIN.

this phenomenon occurs only in cloudy weather and is in reality but the effect of an electrical discharge.

Our pilgrim then, having made his obeisance to these temples on the approach road, passes on his granite way and comes, not heeding a mosque built in memory of one of Aurangzeb's courtiers, at last to the main gate of the temple. The stairway turns a sharp corner suddenly and there, rising high above on a great flight of steps, is the Varah Darwaza—the Gate of Vishnu the Boar—a milk-white arabesqued gateway set in the brown of the fortress wall and overlooked by a quaint abutting window. Inside the great gateway is the first point of pilgrimage—a giant representation of the Varah or Boar incarnation of Vishnu under the belly of which pilgrims must glide if they are to fulfil their obligations. Any one who fails, either by

RAMTEK : THE MUNSAR MANGANESE MINE.

reason of his bulk or from any other cause, to achieve this feat, is deemed a sinner.

Up more steps amid the machicolated walls and the pilgrim passes the Singhpur Gate, and is within the oldest portion of the citadel. Ahead of him is a remarkably picturesque gateway called the Bhairavan Darwaza and guarded by old Mahratta guns. The walls and bastions of this fort were repaired by the Mahrattas in the troublous times when they were making a bid for the Empire of Central India, and are still in the excellent order. And one may look out of their loopholes and through the slits for the weapons of the garrison upon the same scene of wooded fertile country that paid tribute to men long since dust. Below, among the bushes that fringe the natural scarp which was the sole defence of the hill upon this side, grey-whiskered black-faced long-tailed monkeys leap to and fro with much chattering. Within the Bhairava Darwaza rise the chief temples, approached by the Gokul Darwaza which is surmounted by an arch on a platform supported by eight pillars. Through this gate non-Hindus and certain impure castes are not admitted, but from the battlements above the gate can be seen the snowy temples of Lakshman and Rama and Sita with their door plates of brass and silver and their idols of black marble, said to have been miraculously found in a tank after the originals had been mutilated by a Moslem king. An inscription on Lakshman's temple proves that they are six hundred years old.

In and about the temples are all the evidences of an antique citadel; a deep tank approached by many stairways; battlements and loop-holes; tiny doors in deep gateways; and points of vantage to command defence after defence. From a little doorway one looks upon one of those typically Indian scenes that the mind must always remember—a square of wonderfully deep blue sky framed by antique masonry and a vermilion painted image of Hanuman or Ganpat in a stone niche. Never was such a place for shrines and monkeys—there must be hundreds of both. Nor is the catalogue of sacred places yet exhausted for there are still the Bhau Bahin temple of Vishnu in his dwarf incarnation—said to be the oldest temple

RAMTEK: MANGANESE MINING.

MANGANESE MINING: WORKING A CUTTING.

in Ramtek—the Jain "mundils" of Shanti Nath, whose image is eighteen feet long, and the sacred tank of Kinsa, four miles away over the hills.

The great festival of Ramtek occurs in Kartick (November) and lasts fifteen days. Nearly a lakh of pilgrims and sightseers gather and the occasion is made one for a fair at which cloth and utensils are sold. On the principal day a yellow silk cloth, called Pitamber, is burnt at the top of Rama's temple in commemoration of the burning of the demon Tripurasur whom Siva slew.

Apart from its temples Ramtek cuts but a small figure in the world. It grows and exports large quantities of betel-leaf to Madras and Bombay but does little else. The most important commercial concern in the vicinity is the manganese mines of the Central Provinces Prospecting Syndicate, one of the leading firms in the world in this respect. Here it owns two mines—the Kandri and its younger sister the Munsar. Both ship the highest grade ore produced in India and do so in large quantities in normal times.

ON THE ROAD TO RAMTEK.

Visitors to Ramtek may stay at the dak bungalow on Temple Hill, a climb of a mile and a half above the town, but worthy the trouble when its excellent situation and the cool fresh air are taken into account. For the view of the great plains in all their ripe fertility seen beyond the foliage of the hill-trees, of the little square fields with their emerald and golden crops, of copses of great trees, and of the dim blue horizon as the country sleeps beneath the blaze of the sun, is one of the brightest and happiest pictures that India can give.

CHAPTER VII.

In the Kipling Country.

Now Rann the Kite brings home the night
That Mang the Bat sets free—
The herds are shut in byre and hut
For loosed till dawn are we.
This is the hour of pride and power
Talon and tush and claw.
Oh, hear the call ! - Good hunting all
That keep the jungle Law !

NIGHT SONG IN THE JUNGLE.

BLACK night has drawn in upon the jungle fastnesses. Above the dark masses of primeval forest there is no light but the starshine. Within the shadow of the trees, up the rocky shoulder of the ghat, down in the dell by the rippling stream there is darkness ; but not darkness so dense as the human eye imagines. For even the eye of man, removed from the neighbourhood of artificial lights and placed in the dim reaches of forest land will presently recover its lost power of sight in the darkness ; and with the animals, who have never lost the faculty any more than they have the sense of smell, the darkness may be almost as the day. And so the jungle is alive—far more alive now than in the broad light of noon and far more dangerous to the weak. For amid the thickets the creatures of the wild are out on the great business of their life ; to feed and to slake their thirst, Shere Khan, the tiger, is creeping out of his sleeping place, yawning until his ghastly jaws show every terrible tooth ; stretching himself before the stealthy

JUBBULPORE : THE NERBUDDA RIVER.

IN THE KIPLING COUNTRY: CATTLE AND BUFFALO.

stalk that is to bring him a meal. The spotted brothers of Bagheera, the black panther, are preparing for their little excursion to the neighbouring village. If they meet a doe in the jungle well and good—the village is spared its contribution to their larder; if not a goat or a dog will serve. Hathi, the elephant, who is older than many of the men in the jungle can count, rolls silently through the dim aisles of the forest, the saplings springing away from his shoulders, the jungle grass closing again in his wake. The boar have collected on the edges of the tilled lands and are about to feed when the shouts and drumming of the watcher in the lonely thatched machan among the crops and the glow of his signal fire causes them to change their ground. Where the forest stream washes the cool grey rocks with a caressing gurgle and trips lightly past a sandy spit a herd of black buck have come down to drink, with rustling of hoofs, click of horns, a quick alert glance that often goes back over the shoulder, and limbs ready for the dart for safety. A twelve-pointed sambhur scenting Shere Khan, dashes off through the bamboo brakes, horns back on his shoulders, eyes wild with fear. The wolves are out upon the trail and their weird hunting song rises in a great howl above the tree tops;

> As the dawn was breaking the wolf pack yelled
> Once, twice, and again
> Feet in the Jungle that leave no mark!
> Eyes that can see in the dark—the dark!
> Tongue, give tongue to it! Hark, O hark!
> Once, twice and again.

In the little village with its mud walls—a dark patch in a clearing where the stars give a faint light—the cattle have been gathered into the byres, the thorn bushes pulled across the entrance to the stony uneven street and the men gather about the peepul tree while the women tend the bubbling chatties over the glowing home-fires. The pleasant smell of wood smoke fills the air and the wreaths rise high above the thatch-roofs to lie in blue banks in the breathless air. Here in the sheltered village the sounds from the jungle come but faintly, but still the coughing roar of Shere Khan and the faint far howl of a wolf pack on the trail steal out on the silence.

So at least one may picture the scene, for this is the "Kipling Country"; the land of the Seoni wolf-pack and their Council Rock; of Baloo and Bagheera; of Mowgli and Akela, the lone wolf; of the village hunter Buldeo and of the persecuted Messua; of those wonderful stories of wild life that appear in the Jungle Books.

The Kipling Country lies almost anywhere on the narrow gauge system which the Bengal Nagpur Rail-

IN THE KIPLING COUNTRY : QUIET POOLS

IN THE KIPLING COUNTRY : A STATION.

way has laid out in the Central Provinces. The lines run through country that the author had in mind when he was writing that graphic series of stories that tell of the adventures of Mowgli and his brute friends and enemies; when he was giving us those extraordinary revelations into the life of the wild that only his imaginative powers and his knowledge of India could have produced. For here are Seoni, the town which takes its name from the hills in which Mowgli's wolves lived and hunted, and Kanhiwara, the haven of refuge to which Messua and her husband fled after their reception of Mowgli led to the woman being considered a sorceress. Here too, is the Waingunga River, which the Council Rock of the wolves overlooked and at which the beasts of the district drank their fill; the Waingunga which holds the Peace Rock that, bared by the fall of the water after the failure of the rains, is the signal for Hathi to proclaim the Water Truce by which, in those times of dearth and weakness, none may be killed when they come down to the scanty shallows to drink; the Waingunga which boasts the marble rocks and their murderous clusters of Little People over which Mowgli leaped from the jaws of the Red Dogs of the Deccan when the pack, two hundred strong, came down to sweep the Seoni jungle of all living things and found their fate in the stings of the wrathful wild bees and the fangs of the Seoni pack. Here, too, are a hundred little scenes that remind one of Mowgli and his adventures. There lies on many a little eminence a great slab of rock with a circle of lesser stones, and at the base of the hill a little stream which might be the scene which

IN THE KIPLING COUNTRY : THE MARBLE ROCKS.

prompted the appearance of the Council Rock in the Jungle Book. Near Padregunge the youthful Waingunga, here only a few miles from its source in the Seoni district, gives promise of the great stream it is to become ; later it has grown to nearly a mile in width. Continually there are jungles ; the dense scrub jungle such as Shere Khan inhabits ; the high forest trees through the topmost branches of which the Bandar-log carried Mowgli to the City of Cold Lairs ; or through which Mowgli decoyed the Red Dogs to their doom ; jungles in which rocks and bushes and bamboo clumps make a great wilderness ; jungles that climb the precipitous sides of hills, that drop down deep valleys, that clothe level ground. Here and there jungles give way to open land in which Mowgli's village with its ignorant inhabitants and bigoted priest might have been built ; indeed, you may come upon its counterpart with a tumbled collection of houses and mud walls innumerable times. Then, too, there are herds of the slaty-blue great-horned buffalo which Rama, the king of the herd, led to the slaughter of Shere Khan by the Waingunga River, as often as not up to the eyes in a muddy wallow ; scores of cattle grazing on the banks of a stream under the eyes of the village boys ; clusters of agile hungry goats. In the fields rise the thatched "machans" from which the villagers watch their crops at night ; the very type of machan the poles of which Hathi and his sons broke off when they began the grim task of letting in the jungle on Messua's village. Forest streams that tumble overstones and roar wildly among boulders are upon every side. Deep dark pools in which Mowgli and Kaa, the Python,

IN THE KIPLING COUNTRY : A POST RUNNER.

IN THE KIPLING COUNTRY : "THE COUNCIL ROCK."

might have swum together in the moonlight, the boy breaking the moon's reflection with his toes as he floated, gleam cooly beneath a canopy of leaves. Here too, are the people you know best from the illustrations in the "Second Jungle Book" for Mowgli's Men-pack are not largely described with the exception of Buldeo, the hunter, and his Tower musket. But one may recognise the ryot with his pugree twisted and coiled very much over each ear, and the Brahman with his head shaved all except a circle about six inches .n diameter at the crown, thereby reversing the tonsure of the Christian priest. And there will be herd boys of the kind Mowgli domineered when he shepherded the cattle of the village; the children who while away the long days among the buffalo and cattle; weaving little baskets of grass to hold grasshoppers; making two praying mantises fight; singing the long, long native songs with the doleful quaint quaver at the end of a phrase that are so much like a Gregorian chant.

Much of the districts on the narrow gauge may pass for the Mowgli country, for it is all very similar in its jungles, its clearings, its mode of life. The Waingunga River winds its way through the country from its source eleven miles from Seoni, passing Padregung, Keolaree and Balaghat, ever winding and growing until after a course of 360 miles it joins the Wardha to be called the Pranhita and under that name to flow as a tributary of the Godavari, the largest river in Southern India. Seoni, which name will at once recall Mowgli and his jungle friends, is a town so far as the railway is concerned and a very picturesque

IN THE KIPLING COUNTRY WOODCUTTERS AT WORK.

town too, with its antique fort and Jain temple. It is the most important trading town on the Satpura plateau, and with its elevation of 2,233 feet has a delightful climate, free from heat and cold. The nights of the hot weather have the advantage of being cool and pleasant and present an opportunity to recoup from the heat of the day. Jubbulpore, another important centre, the terminus of the line northwards from Gondia, and the junction with the East Indian Railway, has as an attraction some magnificent scenery on the Nerbudda River, where the Marble Rocks are one of the sights of India. Here the river, after a fall of thirty feet, flows for two miles through a channel only twenty yards wide which it has carved for itself from rocks of marble and basalt. The cliffs are 120 feet high. The scene is best viewed at full moon. Here was the site of the Thuggi jail, a part of the work of stamping out one of the most ghastly series of crimes ever conceived or perpetrated.

Balaghat is another large town with many interesting points and one picturesque tank that overlooks the high Satpura hills. Lamta is in the heart of the Satpura Ranges and exports timber and minor forest produce, while it also possesses a temple on a curiously formed hill known as Narsingha. Padreganj is famous for having the Waingunga River flowing a mile distant in the jungles; Nainpur is the junction of the narrow gauge system and will be more important yet when it becomes the headquarters of the Railway officers and the Mandla line is carried to Bilaspur; Chhindwara is one of the healthiest stations of the Central Provinces and is becoming popular as a health resort.

IN THE KIPLING COUNTRY: A TRAVELLING BEGGAR.

NAGBHIR: ON THE NARROW GAUGE.

Of beautiful scenery the narrow gauge district is full; one could hardly imagine a train running through a more romantic land. The line winds through all types of country from the wild forbidding aspect of cliffs that rise perpendicularly to the line to miles of green jungle and the pleasant stretches of the cultivated lands. The best known districts for scenery are the runs between Nainpur and Shikara: between Seoni and Kanhiwara; and between Lamta and Nainpur, but there is not any single stretch or line that is tiresome or monotonous, and the connection of this beautiful district with the works of one

IN KIPLING COUNTRY: A POTTER.

IN THE KIPLING COUNTRY : THE NARROW GAUGE LINE IN THE JUNGLE.

of the greatest story-tellers of the day adds considerably to its attractiveness. Another book which deals with life on the Satpuras is Sterndale's "Seoni, or Camp life on the Satpura Range", a graphic description of the district sixty years ago and full of sporting "gup" and stories. As for sport, the narrow gauge line, like many other parts of the Bengal Nagpur Railway system, presents opportunities for sport unsurpassed in India. All classes of big game are frequent. Many districts are notoriously dangerous at night owing to the presence of tigers. Buffalo and cattle are killed by the score every month, and panthers are repeatedly reported to be carrying off the smaller domestic animals. Bison, nilghai, sambhur and smaller deer and pig are also found. Sportsmen desiring to shoot in the district should communicate with the Deputy Commissioners at Seoni, or at Chhindwara, but the former country supplies the best game. There is also plenty of small game, such as duck and snipe,

IN THE KIPLING COUNTRY : A FOREST STREAM.

pea-fowl, jungle fowl and sand grouse. A permit is necessary for deer but tiger and panther are regarded as vermin and can be shot at any season.

Another section of the narrow gauge line which is of great interest from a scenic point of view is that which runs down to Chanda, an old walled city whose battlements are ten feet thick. They were built by the Gond King, Sir Shah. The town was the capital of the Gond dynasty for six centuries. Here are also tombs of the Gond Rajas and a collection of colossal Hindu deities, the largest of which measures 26 feet. These were prepared for a great temple which was never completed and now lie in a deserted valley.

The Central Provinces of India have excellent roads and many enjoyable motor-trips may be taken along them. There are numerous dak bungalows at which accommodation may be had. A journey such as this would obviously be best taken during the cold weather when the rivers, if unbridged, as a few are, offer no great obstacle. Before planning such a tour it would be advisable to consult the Time Table and Gazetteer issued by the Bengal Nagpur Railway Company.

IN THE KIPLING COUNTRY : PLOUGHING.

RANCHI : TEMPLE HILL.

CHAPTER VIII.

The Charm of Ranchi.

RANCHI is one of those little paradises by which the Indian purgatory is mightily relieved. After the trials of Bengal—the moist days and the moister nights, the humid atmosphere that causes the dweller to exist in a perpetual dampness of body and clothes, the mosquito-infested evenings, and the stillness of the air—the fresh coolth, the dry air, the whispering breezes and the insectless nights of Ranchi are pleasant things. And it owes these blessings to a very small accident when all things are considered; merely to its existence on a plateau two thousand feet high; but those two thousand feet are magic enough to eliminate the whole of the obvious unpleasantnesses of Bengal and to mitigate many of the drawbacks of India as a place of residence.

The sun is hot during the day in the hot season, it is true, but the nights are always cool and pleasant and enjoy a delicious breeze. The rigors of the rains are considerably less than in Bengal. The rainfall is lighter than in the plains proper and only half as much as in Calcutta. In this respect, indeed, Ranchi is better off than some of the more famous hill stations. In the cold weather it retains its charms and the dryness of its air prevents the appearance of that clammy moistness at night that is so disconcerting in the greater part of north-eastern India.

RANCHI : A VIEW FROM TEMPLE HILL.

Ranchi is reached by a pleasant run up hill on a narrow gauge system from Purulia—five hours of journeying among delightful scenery and in a climate that becomes appreciably milder as the engine rounds curve after curve and breasts incline after incline. Here one is among forest-clad eternal hills that lift their fringed tops to make a noble leafy horizon or march their umbrageous glades, their precipitous rocky sides and their little fertile clearings down to the curving line. In the depths of the cuttings, where the jungle makes inviting shade, the air is cool—nearly cold it seems to the traveller used to torrid climes; but withal it is a pleasant coldness reminiscent of bright summer days at Home. Picturesque villages cling to the hill sides and the people are a new sensation; very dark skinned and pleasant featured, with teeth that glisten cheerily in a frequent smile. The women are almost daintily clad in a voluminous saree with broad and narrow borders of red, and the universal adoption of the dress almost suggests a uniform. Both men and women have the pleasant custom of wearing many flowers in their hair, and the spectacle of a tall well-built herdsman with chains of yellow blossoms hanging among his oily ringlets like a cavalier's "love-locks" and accentuating the roguishness of his eyes and the alertness of his features, is a sight to be remembered.

The town itself is pleasant, picturesque in a mild sort of way, and situated in rolling country that might often be mistaken for a stretch of English parkland. The roads are numerous, of excellent surface and well-shaded by avenues of great trees. Motoring here is

RANCHI : THE BENGAL NAGPUR RAILWAY REST HOUSE, OPEN TO VISITORS.

RANCHI : THE CLUB.

exceptionally pleasant, the excellent condition of the thoroughfares for long distances being an unusual feature of the Indian scene. Riding is greatly indulged in, not only along the roads but across country, and a well-supported pack of hounds has been a feature of some seasons. The fact that Ranchi is the summer headquarters of the Government of Bihar and Orissa as well as an important judicial and administrative centre adds to its social amenities. There is a picturesquely-situated Club, with many pucca tennis courts and other sociable features, which extends its membership to visitors under certain conditions. There are golf links and two hotels, of which that of the Bengal Nagpur Railway is very pleasantly situated near the station.

One of the chief sights of the place is Temple Hill, a rugged eminence surmounted by a tiny Hindu temple, that casts its reflection deep into the heart of Tewari tank, a great sheet of water lying along one side of the town. The climb to the top is somewhat of an effort, but once up the traveller is repaid by a stiff and refreshing breeze and by a glorious view of the picturesque country around; a ripe cultivated land, heavily timbered here and there, now with copses, anon with rows of trees that suggest poplars along a road in France, relieved from flatness by many hills. Roads and villages lie out in all directions and the whole prospect is an unusual one for the tropics. Ranchi is one of the smaller show-places of India, it is true, but its charm is not yet widely known. It is, however, becoming more popular and every year the passenger traffic grows a little. It offers a distinctive holiday with amusements that a hill station "pucca" does not possess in its facilities for golfing, hunting and motoring. It is yet in its infancy in this respect but will shortly claim a far greater share of the attention of the healthseeker and holiday-maker from Calcutta.

RANCHI : A SHADY ROAD.

CHAPTER IX.

Southwards from the Hooghly.

EVEN in India, a land of magnificent distances, one slips in travelling from one Presidency or Province into another with a grandiose frequency, meeting rapidly different peoples, customs, dress and language, to say nothing of many changes in scenery and the formation of the earth, with its noticeable effects upon the landscape. From Howrah to Waltair, where the Bengal Nagpur Railway connects with the Madras and Southern Mahratta line to Madras and Ceylon, 547 miles are traversed, in the course of which the line runs from the Presidency of Bengal into the new Province of Bihar and Orissa and finally into the Madras Presidency. Three distinct nationalities occupy the tracts through which the system runs: the Bengalis, who were at one time the conquerors of the land in which they now live; the Ooriyas, a dark-skinned aboriginal race, whose tongue is a notoriously difficult one; and the Telegus, darker still and possessing what is said to be the hardest language to learn in India. The habits, dress, and appearance of all these people are so dissimilar that the ethnological changes alone make the journey of enormous interest.

Above all the type of country is continually changing: new scenes open out on all sides; features that marked one landscape disappear to be replaced by en-

A HERD OF BUFFALO.

A WAYSIDE STATION.

tirely different ones quite as striking in the next; and, what is more, these changes seem to come almost suddenly, as if the scenery had been shifted and the great stage prepared for an entirely new set of characters. He who cannot find delight and enjoyment as the ever changing kaleidoscope of the beauties and wonders of India is thus unfolded before his eyes must indeed, as the old shepherd Corin would say, come of very dull kindred.

Bengal, with its noted climatic conditions of humid heat and heavy rainfall: its panorama of flat flooded paddy fields divided into small squares by "bunds"; its low horizon, always of squat trees; its mud-walled cottages with thatched roofs clustering amid groves of palms; its numerous tanks and full water courses; its cultivators in their scanty dirty white dhoties; its picturesquely draped women passing to the waterside with brass lotas carried on the head or the hip, is as distinct in many respects from Orissa as from Madras. Although similar methods of cultivation exist, there is a marked change in the scenery and people. Hills in Bengal are scarce—non-existent for the most part, but in Orissa the landward or western horizon is one continuous blue chain of hills which run out in spurs until they reach the sea—for the line skirts the coast the whole of the distance to Waltair.

These advance guards of the Eastern Ghauts rise suddenly out of the plain, the nearer ones revealing a rocky surface covered with small scrub and bush. Many of these hump-like hills with their coarse mane of bushes remind one of nothing so much as the Sussex downs: and the higher ones of what passes for

A VILLAGE NEAR CHILKA LAKE.

a mountain in Wales. Approaching Cuttack the whole country-side presents a new appearance. Gone is the kutcha road of Bengal, either inches deep in muddy ruts or glistening with mica; gone is the mud-coloured cottage among the palms; gone is the practically universal cultivation. Here the traveller is in a red land. Laterite out-crops dot the country side, giving a brownish red material for the building of the railway stations, buildings, and bridges, affording red metal for the roads, giving a red tinge to the ryots' huts and even to the people's clothes. A more picturesque scheme in costumes makes its appearance. Dhoties are often of a warm red; the women have a taste in the direction of considerably more variety and brightness. But still the ploughman stands straddle legged upon the wooden plough as he drives his bullocks knee deep in the paddy fields, turns them at impossible angles and never worries in the least as to whether his furrows are straight—so long as he breaks up the earth he is happy.

At Khurda Road one is in the Ooriya country proper. Here nearly every man wears his head shaven to the crown of the skull, while the remaining hair grows long, and is drawn back and then tied into a curious little bob just above the nape of the neck. Clothes if anything become more scanty and a prominent feature in the fields is the great circular hat of palm leaves rising to a point in the centre and tied over the pugri and under the chin. The dress of the women has been completely changed. Here the majority wear a sad coloured yellow cloth that harmonises strikingly with their complexions; gold ornaments are stuck in the

CHILKA LAKE.

A BOAT ON THE CHILKA LAKE.

nose and ears; the anklet has disappeared, but every woman boasts a series of bell metal bracelets that occupy the arm from the wrist nearly to the elbow. The dress is worn much shorter and sometimes a reddish border seems to accentuate the display of knee and thigh.

The face of the country has been altering also. The trees have become in many cases greater and more spacious; villages are hidden away in the folds of little areas of woodland and only peep out coyly, as it were, from behind a wealth of foliage. Hills and rocky out-crops have become still more prominent and the horizon to landward is entirely filled with a great confusion of dim blue shapes. On the east of the line there has arrived that curious appearance of the land ending in the air which tells of the presence of the sea, and at Bhusandpur the great stretches of Chilka Lake lie out like a sheet ot glass beneath the blazing sky.

"KILLARNEY" ON CHILKA LAKE.

Chilka Lake is a natural phenomenon due, in the chief instance, to the never-ceasing fight between the river and the land on a flat shore. Originally it was a portion of the Gulf of Bengal and presumably the surf that beats all along the beaches of Orissa—except here and there where the hills come down to form an ironbound coast—once boomed and resounded where now the cattle graze on the edge of still water that scarcely knows a ripple. But the silt-bringing rivers, fighting with the sand-heaping sea have barred the entrance to the Chilka Lake until not only has it been almost closed, but a great bar has been flung up that few boats can cross. The land is achieving a victory over the sea on this coast. Records show that not only has a mile or so of blown sand been heaped up along the coast, but that the fertile paddy fields of Orissa were once the sea bottom, and that the hills that occur so frequently in the landscape were formerly islands such as now rise out of the Chilka Lake. That majestic sheet of water is now an inland sea, dotted with islets of all sizes and consisting in formation not only of grass covered mounds but of rocky cliffs that climb to a considerable height.

The scenery on the Chilka Lake rises to heights of great beauty and is of all types, from the typically Indian product of the Nalabari or reed forest, to an inlet at Rambha hedged in by great hills that has been likened to the Lakes of Killarney. And, indeed, seen amid the soft rain of a drizzling day in the monsoon the hills opposite Rambha fully deserve that happy comparison.

Rambha was formerly a popular resort of the European community at Ganjam in the days of the Honourable Company and when that little station was of some importance in the world. The Raja of Kallikota has three residences in this District, one inland from the station of that name, another at Rambha, overlooking the lake and a third on an island in the centre commanding a glorious view of the inland sea. This residence was built by a former official of the Company named Snodgrass, about whom many stories are told. One of the best is that Snodgrass shook the pagoda tree to such an extent that even John Company felt compelled to recall him. On his return to London he became at once the injured servant and pleaded poverty to such an extent that he sat on the doorstep of the Company, literally in rags, until, out of self-respect the Directors presented him with a pension to be paid monthly. And on the day

THE VILLAGE BARBER.

GANJAM: THE OLD CEMETERY.

when the first remittance was due he drove up to draw it tooling a magnificent four-in-hand! A dak bungalow at Barkal is famous for presenting one of the finest stretches of lake scenery.

According to tradition the Chilka was formed by an inrush of the sea, and the legend blends fairly well with the stories of the destruction of Pharoah's army in the Red Sea and of Canute. In the fourth century it is said, a strange race came across the sea to sack the temple at Puri. The priests, surmising the threatened danger from the litter of elephants and horses that the tide brought ashore, hurried the idols off inland. The invaders, enraged with the tell-tale ocean, determined to attack the sea. As they marched against them, the waters treacherously retreated for two miles and then surged back upon their presumptuous pursuers, swallowed them, and in their mad delight at victory, flooded a great portion of the district of Puri and formed the Chilka Lake.

Passing these picturesque landscapes the line has been executing tortuous turns and sailing up and down among the hills. At last it reaches Ganjam, now almost a town of the dead, but at one time a populous settlement. Now all that exists are relics of a past glory—a ruined fort and a grave-yard. Time was when the city was almost famous. At that date it was well built, even in the Indian quarter, and although the houses are a hundred and twenty years old they are still used as residences by the descendants of the people who survived the great scourage of fever that either carried off or frightened away 24,000 people between 1815 and 1818. The town was well laid out

GANJAM : THE RUINED COMMANDANT'S HOUSE.

GANJAM : THE GATE AND MOAT.

with exceptionally broad streets: the houses are built with over-hanging eaves supported on pillars or posts, often gaily coloured. But only a few of these are inhabited, many are in ruins, and the streets are grass-grown and covered with debris. The city is, indeed, a graveyard of the past for the most part. Its Bara Bazar is a desolate grassy waste with a few ruins of Indian shops and a wrecked obelisk; a deserted mosque—there is now not a Mohamedan in the place —has stood the action of time and weather better than many other buildings; bridges and culverts have fallen into chaos. All that is left of the European settlement is the graveyard and the ruined fort. The cemetery contains a number of tombs, the earliest dated 1774 and the latest 1893. This last is an exceptional case for the inscription records the death of a sailor who was killed in 1893 while landing the first cargo of railway material imported at that point. All the epitaphs with this exception are dated between 1774 and 1820. It was about the latter date that the settlement, owing to the fever that ravaged the town, was moved to Chatrapur, a few miles to the south.

The fort is of fair extent but has fallen sadly from its former magnificence. The moat has shrunk to a pool or two; the drawbridge has gone; the gateways are choked by prickly pear and shrubs; the central building—presumably the Commandant's house—is a mere shell. Half a mile away from both these relics the white surf of the sea breaks on the sandy beach, and its roar strikes the ear like a booming death knell for the settlement and a warning of the mutability of man's power and prowess.

Beyond Ganjam, at a little station called Mandasa Road, is a beautiful rock temple which is worth inspecting. But as it is fifteen miles distant and on the crest of the highest hill within view the journey is made with the assistance of a hill tribe who carry up the visitor.

Naupada has the distinction of possessing large salt pans leased out to makers by the Salt Department. The pans lie out in a huge circle some miles in circumference and the interior stretch of water is broken up with bunds in the manner of rice fields. Salt water enters from the sea by a small channel from which it flows into different shallow enclosures where the water evaporates. A crust of salt of about three inches in height is left after the third series of operations. This is scraped off the bed of the pans,

PUNDI : A WEEKLY MARKET.

PUNDI : ON THE WAY TO MARKET.

IN MADRAS : TEA GARDEN COOLIES RETURNING.

and stored in "platforms," of which there are five, and then weighed into maunds and roofed in with straw. Here it is sold to buyers and the Government takes a rupee for every maund. The pans are strongly guarded and during the manufacturing season—the hot weather—a large force of armed peons are always on duty and watch-men have their posts elevated on high poles above each "platform." The salt stored under the straw consists of coarse dirty-looking crystals.

By this time the land of the Telegus has been reached. As this is one of the hottest districts in India, the fact that the ryot puts most of his clothing on his head is no matter for wonder. Nearly every one carries a huge umbrella of palmyra leaves under which he squats, whether tending his buffaloes, driving a bullock cart, or transplanting paddy. The women wear their brilliantly coloured clothes more simply than the races further North, do not cover the head, and cross the saree over the right shoulder instead of the left. The huts are circular and thatched with that useful article, the broad palmyra leaf, which is used for so many purposes as to be indispensable to the majority of the poorer classes.

By now the country has changed again. Still the Eastern Ghauts run with the Railway, but they have increased in height and are often formed of great boulders of slaty rock; others again are of a deep red colour. Near Chicacole Road a most interesting natural phenomenon in a series of great rocky outcrops—boulder upon boulder piled to a great height—comes down close to the line. The earth is a rich red ; huge conglomerations of red and purplish rocks dot the fields and edge the little pools ; and the palmyra trees with their straight trunks and little tufts of green fan-shaped leaves at the top—all as much alike as uniformed soldiers—grow in thousands on every hand. The date trees that cluster amid full-leaved bushes and trees in little patches of jungle ; the red earth of the fields ; the sand of the roads and uncultivated spaces ; the armies of palmyra trees ; the great blue hills and the azure sky ; the herds of slow blue-skinned buffalo ; the roofed in bullock-garis with their milkwhite kine ; and the people—men and women—bending over their work in the paddy fields make up a picture which is in truth the India of one's dreams.

Vizianagram is one of those deceptive places that is much bigger and of far more importance than it looks. When one reads that the town boasts an old fort built by Bussy, the famous French soldier of fortune, one may be prepared to find it something like Ganjam. But no expectation could be more incorrect. Far from being a dead city Vizianagram is alive and very much kicking. Not only has it already a growing trade in a large variety of country produce, but it is making a name for itself in jute. In the jute season the station never rests and despatches load after load of the raw material. One press is already in existence and another is shortly to be built.

Perhaps, however, Bussy's Fort and the Palace of the Maharaja of Vizianagram which it encloses will remain the chief item of interest to visitors. The old black battlements with their round corner bastions and their

VIZIANAGRAM : THE TEMPLE.

ramparts pierced for big guns stand on the bank of a picturesque lake. These staunch old walls, however, are all that remain of the fortress. The interior is occupied by the Palace and its beautiful gardens which, however, is only one of some half-dozen residences of His Highness. Another is to be seen on the highest point of the highest hill in the district and can be clearly observed through a telescope placed in the drawing-room of the fortress-palace.

The residence within the fort contains a large number of old arms—spears, muzzle-loaders and swords used in an eighteenth century battle between the Maharaja's followers commanded by Bussy, and those of the Maharaja of Bobbili. A small force of the French General had been cut up by the Bobbili troops. Bussy went out on a punitive expedition and practically exterminated Bobbili and its inhabitants. There are

VIZIANAGRAM : THE WALL OF THE PALACE.

also on exhibition arms presented to the Maharaja by Queen Victoria and the late King; several busts and portraits of the heads of the house; a suite of red velvet and silver furniture; and many models and pictures. In fact the drawing-rooms of the Palace comprise a museum and art gallery that have many objects worthy of attention.

The town has a large bazar, two or three temples, a Municipal park and a veterinary establishment maintained by the Maharaja, where horses and cattle are treated free.

Any one who has made such a journey as is here described will have no doubt of the delights and interest of travelling in India. In addition to historical and modern centres to be visited there is much to be seen during the actual passage of the train. The line always runs so close to the people that the country is, as it were, taking one into its confidence as to the daily round and common task of its races; revealing a strange and, to some eyes, romantic life. In no other land does the railway seem to play so great a part in the welfare of the nation. Railways in Britain and Europe are haughty distant organisations that hurry you along through cuttings and high embankments without granting you more than a glimpse of a man ploughing or the wash drying in the back garden. In India a railway takes you by the hand and shows you the different people of a vast Empire at their various tasks; in their little villages; at their fairs; and on their holidays. Not only this, but the Company deals with its Indian travellers in a fatherly sort of way, shepherding them on the platform and into the trains with no hurry and bustle and with an air that there is plenty of time. And yet things are not done so inexpediently after all. Old men and women with much paraphernalia and many children and young men and their wives and an only off-spring alike are got safely in and out of trains with extraordinary rapidity, and the station is cleared long before there appeared any hope of a move, considering the motley assembly in view when it was reached. And every one, it seems, is happy. The Indians squat on their benches and on the top bunks with cheery faces, sunny smiles and much talk-

VIZIANAGRAM : THE CLOCK TOWER.

VIZIANAGRAM : THE MAHARAJA'S PALACE.

ing and gesticulating. Any one can see that the ride to them is a pleasure jaunt. But how they sort out their multitudious belongings must always remain a mystery.

After all the chief appeal to the *voyageur* on these journeys is always the little glimpses of a new life to him; and yet a life as old as the hills to the people of the place. Here, for instance, is the weekly bazar in progress at a tiny station in Madras. Long before you approach the stopping place, you see hundreds of people, all carrying burdens, trooping along the side of the line to the "hat". Lithe red-robed women bearing fish in rush baskets, ghee in black chatties, or milk in pans, stride with a fine grace and swing along the sandy pathway; a small herd of cattle with the driver (beneath a huge palm topee) guiding them with a long stick, shuffle gently along; a bullock cart heaped high with chillies and fruits rumbles by, the driver under an umbrella of leaves; scores of children troop past, many mites bearing bravely and with extraordinary skill their share of the produce of the little

NAUPADA : THE SALT PANS.

NAUPADA : A SALT PLATFORM.

farm. All over the countryside, as far as the eye can see, similar parties are approaching along narrow foot-paths through the fields, like flies making for a honeypot. The bazar itself is a wild conglomeration of sellers squatting among their goods. Every one seems to be selling and never buying, but you suppose that in the end the *mucheewallah* will buy ghee from the *gwala*, while the *gwala* will take home a few fish, and so on. If not trade would be at a standstill.

There are always the pictures in the widespread fields, full of happy labour, and the picturesqueness of man's oldest industry—the tilling of the soil. A whole village transplanting in the paddy fields—the men, balancing on their wooden shares, ploughing in the flooded square plots, the women, a motley coloured crowd, with many a flash of bangle and earring in the sun, bending to their

MANGANESE MINING IN THE CENTRAL PROVINCES: LOADING WAGONS AT TUMSAR ROAD.

work of dibbling in the tender rice plants; a herd of buffalo up to the eyes and nostrils in water, placidly chewing the cud; another grazing near by in couples, the herdsman sitting sideways on one of a pair, or giving an impromptu circus exhibition by standing upright on the broad quarters of the beast; a herd of goats nibbling busily under the eye of a wee child wearing a sun hat big enough for his grandfather; a string of burdened travellers fording a flooded river above the knees in swirling water; a man coming waist deep through a crop of Indian corn, are but a few of the fascinating pictures that the mind carries after a railway journey in India.

When the darkness has settled down and the land lies out under the starshine and the dim black hills seemed to have marched in closer until they hem the world around, a million noise-weaving creatures wake to life. Stopping at a station, and sometimes through the roar of the train, one hears the gutteral song of the frogs under wet banks in an undertone of croaks, while one big fellow near by adds a solo akin to the throbbing of a drum; high above the drone of the frogs is the whirr of insects and the high chirping of the crickets in their unseen choirs. Lights twinkle among the fields—the signal of village homes or a lamp that lights the wayfarer on a lonely road. From the station a little party is setting out for their village keeping well together, lighting their way with many lanterns, and singing as they go. And the sound of their voices comes across the still fields until the train moves on, but after the music of their chant has died away for long the lights of their lamps twinkle among the blackness in the shadow of the great hills.

CHAPTER X.

Cuttack—Its Past and Present.

CUTTACK, like many another town both large and small on the Eastern Coast of the Indian Peninsula, had its share in the history of the early English occupation of India. The uphill fight of the East India Company to obtain commercial recognition in Bengal and the districts subject to the rulers of that rich Province began at Hariharpur, a tiny settlement between Cuttack and the sea. And Hariharpur, be it noted, possessed the first English factory founded north of what is now the Madras Presidency.

The first traders in Bengal had many disadvantages to combat, difficulties to overcome, and battles to fight. Every attempt of theirs to obtain a foothold was resented by the Dutch, the Portuguese and the French, and more than mere persuasion was used to prevent designs becoming accomplished facts. Thus, when the English factory at Masulipatam sent a small expedition northward to open up trade in Bengal, a Portuguese man-o'-war followed. Only eight Englishmen sailed in this venture, and their craft was little better than a country boat that could offer but little resistance to the weather and none at all to armed enemies. Slowly the little galleon, bent on an errand that was to help in founding an Empire—although neither Robert Cartwright, who headed it, nor any

CUTTACK : MAHANADI BRIDGE AND FERRY.

of his men had such a thought in their adventurous heads—crept along the coast until it reached the giant estuary of the Mahanadi—that great river that drains the ghauts of the Central Provinces and sweeps to the sea in mile-wide torrents. On the 1st of April 1633, Cartwright cast anchor at Harishpuragur with as much pomp as possible and with a brave display of best clothes on the part of himself and his companions—silk doublets, a little tarnished may be by the eastern suns but still reminiscent of the Pool of London, befeathered hats, and huge yellow boots—prepared to land to interview the "Ragger," who according to the Captain's log, controlled the custom house and the fort of Harishpuragur. For the Moguls in those days let no means of taking tribute escape them, and both imports and exports contributed their mites to the kingly coffers. The "Ragger"—of course, we should spell his name Raja now—agreeably condescended to receive the English, and Robert Cartwright already imagined himself the head of a new factory when a sail appeared on the horizon. As it crept inshore, the Portuguese colours were flown at the peak, Not to be outdone, Cartwright, who was one of your daredevil fellows, ran up the English flag—then as much of the Union Jack

A SCENE IN CUTTACK.

as England and Scotland could make between them. This rather annoyed the "Portugee" and she sailed into port, anchored in dangerous proximity to the English ship, and ostentatiously ran out a gun or two. Nothing daunted, the English went ashore. The Portuguese crew followed and like Roderigo in the affair with Cassio, put an affront on Cartwright and his men. Swords were drawn and a very pretty European brawl took place in the local Burra Bazar, in which the English, being sadly outnumbered, began to get the worse of it. Lakshmi Raja, who must have been a sportsman—at least his sympathies were with the smaller party—turned out with two hundred men and prevented the English being "slained or spoiled."

Cartwright, not to be outdone, travelled inland to interview the Mahomedan Governor of Orissa, who held his court at Cuttack. Here, too, the Portuguese Captain followed, and here another entertaining little scene occurred in the Governor's presence, Cartwright claiming redress for the Portuguese attack upon him and the Portuguese lodging a cross case. The Governor, who was something of a Solomon as well as having an eye to the main chance, confiscated both boats. Cartwright, his high spirit rising at this injustice "rose up and departed saying that if he could not have right here he would have it in another place. And so (says the ship's log laconically) he went his way, not taking leave of the Nawab or any other, at which abrupt departure they all admired."

The Governor took it all in good part. He let Cartwright cool his heels; and Cartwright waited too. In three days' time the Governor made the first advance. He sent for Cartwright, who came with a "stern and undaunted countenance" under his plumed hat, and gave the Nawab a piece of his mind to the effect that His Highness had done great injustice which his masters were not likely to brook. The Governor appealed to his court as to "what sort of a nation it was that bred men like that"—a form of query that is familiar in India to this day. The Nawab's court evidently knew more than he, and they told him that Cartwright represented a nation that was invincible on the sea. After that the Governor thought better of things and gave Cartwright his firman to trade and sped the parting guest with a banquet.

Then the new factory was built at Hariharpur and was for some time of considerable importance to the Company. That it never rose to prominence is probably due to the uncertainty of the Mahanadi, which is a comparative trickle in the dry season although it floods the countryside in the rains.

Cuttack itself is built at the apex of the delta of the river, and in order to prevent the city following its environs into the swollen flood, a great stone embankment has been constructed to enable the spit of sand upon which Cuttack stands to face the devastating tides.

But without penetrating to the far side of Cuttack the traveller can see the enormous difficulties which the swelling of the Mahanadi threaten and especially those which confronted the engineers when the Bengal Nagpur line came to be built across Robert Cartwright's old route to Cuttack. Between Jagatpur and

CUTTACK : THE "DOCK" FOR INLAND TRAFFIC.

Barang, a distance of only ten miles, the line crosses three great river beds, the Mahanadi, the Kathjuri and the Khorkai. The traveller in the dry season sees on either hand of these bridges but vast stretches of glistening sand with here and there a pool or a rivulet. The bed of the river is criss-crossed with tracks of coolies who carry loads from a ferry at one deep place in the channel to another ; of herds passing to and fro ; of the general traffic of the country. Here many a bullock-cart draws a load of rice across the sandbanks, its wheels sinking inches deep ; there a ferry boat with a motley crowd of country people and a couple of bullocks aboard, poles slowly to the further bank. The channels are often only an eighth of the breadth of the river-bed and even the great Mahanadi is only a shadow of the might it possesses in the rains. The Khorkai is more often little more than a chain of pools. But in the monsoon when every rivulet is pouring its spate into the streams, and the streams are filling the twenty feet high banks of the river, the flood runs furlongs wide. The bridge over the Mahanadi at Cuttack is at present the fifth largest bridge in India, being one and a fifth miles in length. Indeed it is claimed that between Jagatpur and Barang the iron road is carried over perhaps the most difficult piece of riverine engineering in India. Time was when the old East Coast Railway, built as a famine works by Government, ended at Barang, but that was before the Bengal Nagpur Railway experts got to work. Since the bridging of this quartette of rivers the journey between Bengal and Madras has been reduced by thirty-eight hours along the East Coast seaface.

Another prominent feat of riverine engineering is the anicut which has been built by the P. W. D. on the Mahanadi to keep the canals to their proper level and also to "train" the river to a certain extent. Here a set of sluice gates and cement work stretches nearly three quarters of the way across the stream. The pent-up river pours through the openings in the cement bund in a boiling cataract of yellow waves that fling up a curling crest of muddy spume when the waters reach their new level.

The Bengal Nágpur Railway has also done many other things for Cuttack. The countryside here is served by canals and communication is made over hundreds of miles by country boats. Imports for Orissa and the Central Provinces as far as Raipur come in small vessels to Chandbali, there they are transhipped into river steamers, and again distributed into the

CUTTACK : THE ANICUT.

long, highly painted boats that can go almost anywhere. A large point for distribution has been erected at Cuttack in the shape of a dock—or rather a deep tank that runs alongside a freight yard. Here goods are imported and exported. The success of the undertaking is seen from the fact that a few years ago only five merchants had godowns on the shores of this "dock"; to-day thirty have their warehouses there and building is still going on.

Cuttack itself is a prosperous place, and prosperity and cleanliness are written upon its streets. The roads are of the rich-coloured red laterite that is so prominent in this part of India, and they present a splendid surface after the sand-coloured dusty or muddy—as the case may be—thoroughfares of Bengal. Trade is developing and in addition the local workmen fashion curiosities out of horn and do good work in woodcarving.

CHAPTER XI.

The Village of a Hundred Shrines.

ALTHOUGH from the railway line on the far side of Bhubaneswar from Calcutta the towers of many temples rise against the sky, indicating the existence of numerous shrines, there is at the station no indication of greatness or interest of any kind apart from the general suggestion of the homely life of the ryot with its primitive simplicity and apparently immovable placidity. Bhubaneswar is like any other of the smaller stations on the line—a little building half-hidden by trees and backed by a cluster of mud-huts and the full foliage of the jungle. Not a spire or dome rises on the horizon of low tree growths ; not a sign appears of the glories long departed. And yet, say some authorities, for six centuries Bhubaneswar was the capital of the Siva-worshipping Kings of the Kesari or Lion dynasty of Orissa. Thousands of pilgrims flocked to these holy shrines before St. Augustine landed to preach the White Christ to the Angles ; the roads to Bhubaneswar were crowded at puja times while Alfred the Great was spoiling the cakes in the neatherd's hut, while Harold was fighting his last great fight beneath the dragon standard on the hill of Senlac, while Henry II was scourging himself before the tomb of Thomas à Becket. From A. D. 500 to 1130, say

BHUBANESWAR : THE GREAT TANK AND LINGARAJ TEMPLE.

some versions of the matter, the Kesari kings lavished all the wealth of artistic talent at their command—and incidentally some of the finest the world has ever produced—upon the architecture and decoration of the seven thousand shrines that once clustered about the sacred lake of Bhubaneswar. Opinions differ again as to the number of temples in the sacred area of three miles that is to-day called Bhubaneswar, but, however many there were in the past, there are to-day about a hundred—some of them deserted and almost in ruins. But the traveller will not be likely to take sides in any discussion as to whether the Kesari kings built the temples or not. Indeed one writer holds that there was no such thing as the Kesari dynasty much less a rule by it in Orissa for six hundred years. But the past of this portion of India is so dimmed by the mists of the past that no circumstantial history is extant. The chief point, however, is that the temples still remain and that they prove the existence in India fifteen centuries ago of marvellous architectural skill combined with extraordinary workmanship and an ability for artistic sculpture that was not perhaps equalled in the world at that date and has rarely been surpassed since. Just as surprising is the fact that these ancient builders, whoever they were, contrived to manœuvre huge blocks of stone into position at enormous heights; to keep them in place without any mortar or fastening; and, what is more, to give them a permanent stability that has outlived for centuries the stress of Indian winds, the fierce violence of the Indian rains, and the worst efforts of cyclonic forces. Even to this day, while the figures are in some cases worn away and

BHUBANESWAR : THE BEAUTIFUL TEMPLE OF MUKTESWAR.

disfigured by the weather, dainty arabesques and flower pattern borders and a sort of sturdy lace-work remains perfect, with sharp corners and shapes nearly as cleanly cut as when the sculptor laid down his chisel so many hundreds of years ago.

The sacred portion of Bhubaneswar is a little troublesome to reach but it is well worthy of pains and tribulations when one arrives. The place is innocent of garis as the ultra-civilised person knows them; the only equipage for the road here is the byle-gari—and the humble bullock cart, jolty, slow, archaic vehicle as it is, has to be accepted. You will probably descend the little slope that runs down from the station at a trot, the bullocks responding cheerfully to the usual complicated indications to "chelo" provided by the gari-wallah. But that little burst sees them more or less spent and thereafter you feel that it is a life-and-death struggle to get them to put one leg before the other. Your driver shrieks and hoicks at the top of his voice; murmurs rudely, in a guttural undertone, long sentences in which the same words are often repeated; resorts even to casting reflections upon the parents of the beast. Another method of increasing the pace—and a more effective one than the use of the voice—is tail-twisting and a stick plucked at the moment from a bush by the roadside. Clouts from this goad fall like drum-rolls and even a protest from the sahib inside the gari produces little effect. Perhaps the bullock driver as a general rule is more merciful than he appears—for the driver will pretend to goad the animal in the ribs with the business end of the stick, but you notice that he stops short and is only desirous

BHUBANESWAR : THE OLDEST EXISTING TYPE OF ORISSAN ARCHITECTURE.

of bluffing the bullocks in order to urge them onwards without further punishment. The trouble is, however, that they refuse to be bluffed.

The journey to Bhubaneswar's shrines is unusually monotonous but, as has been said, the temples are worth while when the experience is at an end. When you catch your first sight of Bhubaneswar as seen across the sacred tank of Vindusagar, said to contain drops from all the sacred rivers and tanks in India, you forgive the gari-wallah for having jolted you to pieces in his anxiety to pass other carts by deviations round the sides of steep banks at a trot, and feel almost genial towards the matting roof of the gari in spite of several attacks upon your topi. For out of the centre of a great lake embanked by dark red laterite and with shores broken by numerous bathing ghats juts a tiny island with two milk white temples casting their reflections into the still waters. Behind them rise the great carved towers of the principal temple, the Lingaraj and its neighbour the Bhagavarti. Many other ribbed domes flank the principal spire, but there is only one Lingaraj and its spire is always the centre of the landscape.

No European is allowed to enter even the compound of the Lingaraj, but some thoughtful person has erected a platform as high as the walls themselves so that those who are not of the faith may obtain some glimpse of the glories of Orissan architecture of the past. In the flagged space about the greatest temple with its carved verticals and its characteristic lion rampant on an elephant projecting from the side of the spire rise between sixty and seventy smaller temples or shrines. Each of these is a work of art by the sculptor, but the mind and eye always go back to the enormous Lingaraj with its majestic proportions, its extraordinary means of construction, the ornamentation that crowds its entire exterior, but yet never presents the appearance of being overdone.

Perhaps the scene from the walls is far more impressive and effective than it would be were one in the midst of the crowd in the courtyard; for here one may watch the worshippers pouring up a broad flight of steps and through a majestic doorway; children dancing about the smaller shrines; and, in fact, something of the inner life of the temple.

The next most prominent temple in Bhubaneswar is Mukteswar, one of the smallest, but one of the most

BHUBANESWAR : THE LINGARAJ TEMPLE.

artistic and beautiful in decorations and general conception. The ornamentation of the porch-roof is unusual and this non-Hindus are admitted to see. The general appearance of the exterior is made the more impressive by the elaborate archway that stands before the entrance. The decorations of the walls of the Mukteswar temple are more artistic and varied and less gross than usual. The female figures appear playing musical instruments or dancing; an emaciated hermit gives lessons in discipline; elephants fight with lions; a lady mounted on a rearing elephant strikes at a giant with a sword; while the scrolls, figures and flower patterns that fill in the design until not an inch of the walls is left plain prove marvellous skill in execution. Mukteswar, indeed, is the gem of the whole Bhubaneswar collection.

Parasurameswar, a much-restored temple standing lonely and far distant from any neighbour, is said to be the oldest existing temple in the whole of Orissa. It is, however, less ornate and every much smaller than some. Its age is the chief point of interest, for it is also the oldest example of the characteristic architecture of the period.

Bhubaneswar has other remains. At Dhauli, four miles away, there are rock edicts of Pryadasi and Asoka, while immediately above these is said to be the oldest carving of an elephant in India. This is now worshipped by the Hindus in honour of Ganesh, the elephant-headed god of war, although originally designed as an emblem of Gautama Buddha.

Bhubaneswar has not only declined in historical fame but also in religious appreciation. To-day only a few of the thousands who attend the great festivals

BHUBANESWAR : A RICHLY CARVED TEMPLE.

at Puri go to Bhubaneswar. Many stay only a few hours, and the income of the priests has dwindled to scantiness. But the great interest of the temples is the gradual evolution which they present of that peculiar style of Hindu architecture known as Orissan. The Puri district alone contains the best examples of this school. The art began with the temple of Parasurameswar and reached its meridian in the majestic structures of Lingaraj and Jagannath at Puri. It closed with the now ruined Sun Temple at Konarak. The grandeur of the buildings, the elaboration of the minutest details, the gigantic size of the stone blocks and iron beams used, the fact that not an atom of mortar was used in construction, and the exquisite carvings on stone so hard that it has withstood ten centuries of the winds, rains and suns of India, combine to justify the statement that the Orissan temples provide "one of the most complete and interesting styles of Indian achitecture."

CHAPTER XII.

The Khandagiri Caves.

AMONG the most interesting and ancient remains of the Bhubaneswar district are a number of Jain caves in the hills of Khandagiri. These date back to the third century B.C., and are held to be, owing to their number, age and carvings, the most interesting in Eastern India. Khandagiri presents difficulties of access but with the aid of a motor car it is easily accessible from Bhubaneswar, and may even be reached by bullock cart, although the time occupied would be considerable. If a trip by car is in contemplation it should not be made during or immediately after the rains as the passage of the stream Kochilakhunta by a ford then presents difficulties. The road from Bhubaneswar leads straight to Khandagiri after crossing the railway, dips to the level of the Kochilakhunta, and rises again gradually to the hill, which with its temple has been in sight throughout the journey. There are three peaks to the hill—Udayagiri or the Sunni Hill with 44 caves; Khandagiri, or the Broken Hill with 19 caves, and Nilgiri, or the Blue Hill, with three caves.

Udayagiri, while possessing the greatest number of caves, has also the largest and most interesting. This is the Ranihansapura or Raninabara cave ; that is to say the Queen's Palace. It contains two ranges of caves

KHANDAGIRI : THE QUEEN'S PALACE.

on three sides of a quadrangle, with the south-east side open to the jungle. The caves consist of rooms carved out of the living rock and ornamented with numerous figures, scenes and symbols. At the end of each long verandah of caves stands on guard a figure. That on the lowest is a soldier with clothes worn like a wrestler, a spear in the right hand and a coil of rope in the other. In the upper wing the guards are the goddess Amba on a lion and Indra on a bull or elephant. In the upper right wing kilted soldiers stand armed. There are low stone benches in the caves—a feature but little found elsewhere—and the roofs of various verandahs are supported by pillars. Many of the originals have disappeared and those that remain seem to be in the last stage of decay. The missing supports have now been replaced by modern pillars for preservative purposes. These show clear white and make no pretence at decoration.

The carvings in these caves are of especial interest and they have been the cause of much keen discussion among archæologists. One of the principal presents the procession of a saint through a town during a religious festival. There are many little pictures in the frieze. One represents people looking from the windows of a house ; another figures carrying umbrellas and riding horses and elephants—three men on one beast ; a third a family going to make offerings at a temple ; a fourth caparisoned led horses and guards and so on.

A second frieze is yet more interesting and illustrative of ancient India. From under rocks come elephants apparently hunted by both men and women with ropes. Another scene shows a combat between a male and a lady both armed with a short sword and spear, and ends in the lady being carried off bodily by the male. Another series depicts hunting, showing a prince about to mount a horse held by a boy and attended by four men with straight swords. Later the prince shoots at a winged deer and talks with a lady. Then a feast is shown and an amorous scene between a male and a female. It is held that these figures depict scenes in the life of Parsvanath, a noted Jain saint, and a son of the King of Benares. According to mediæval lore, Parsvanath rescued a beautiful princess after she had been abducted by a Kalinga king and was given her hand in marriage. Ultimately he became an ascetic.

KHANDAGIRI : A CAVE.

The frieze shows the story of these incidents in his life.

Among the numerous other caves inscriptions as well as carvings exist, but in many of these letters are missing. Yet on being deciphered they have yielded valuable information. On the other hand the Queen's cave contains no inscriptions. Very much the same story as is told in its friezes is, however, repeated in the Ganesha cave on the same hill. One of the inscriptions is the famous pronouncement of King Kharavala which dates the cave in which it appears at between 150 and 153 B. C. A distinctive cave is one called the Bagha-gumpha or Tiger's mouth, which is mostly natural and presents a very fair idea of a tiger's head with open jaws.

Khandagiri hill contains a two-storeyed cave, much damaged by the weather which is more imposing than most. The carvings are rude but vigorous, and figures of animals—elephants for instance—are particularly good. There are many pictures of domestic life and objects used in both out-door and in-door life are depicted, providing the archæological student with valuable material. The top of Khandagiri Hill proper has been levelled and a Jain temple built, but this is comparatively recent.

CHAPTER XIII.

The God and the Lover.

THE pious Hindu and his women folk and children, when they set out to visit the sacred places in Puri, have a round of visits to pay to many deities before they see the great Jagannath and his brother and sister ride from their home in the "White Pagoda" at Puri to the Garden of Pleasure. Many devotees visit the shrines at Satyabadi, and subsequently they may go to Bhubaneswar. Both are within easy reach of the railway line and not far from "the city," as ancient chronicles speak of Puri. Satyabadi with its great temple to Krishna is the easier to come to and is the pleasantest of walks from the station of Sakhigopal. The road from the station to the temple turns to the left over a level crossing and then proceeds under a great shady avenue of trees into the heart of the little settlement. Passing a large picturesque walled store-yard that indicates one reason for the existence of the village—it is the centre of the local trade in cocoanuts—the shady road runs into a little open space surrounded by the ordinary village residences but far more picturesque than usual. The mud verandahs seem more spacious, the huts more commodious, the palm trees in greater profusion. There is an air of cleanliness and alertness that is usually absent from Indian villages. Over a neat stone bridge comes in

SAKHIGOPAL : THE TEMPLE.

sight a picturesque bathing tank with several ghats. In the centre rises two small white shrines that reflect their dainty contours in the placid waters. On the opposite bank stands a much decorated ghat and near it a little rest house for pilgrims which at certain times is crowded with devotees. Round the tank bends the road and then a long avenue of palms opens out. Through the luxuriant foliage of a beautiful garden, the tower of the temple—white against the blue sky—dominates the scene. The approach road is lined by rest houses and residences, and at last, bursting upon the sight as one rounds a curve, leaps into the air the temple with its antecedent sun pillar and its carved and painted entrance. The main building, which is seventy feet high, is an admirable illustration of Orissan architecture and its richly carved ribbed dome shows the usual features of a lion rampant on an elephant projecting from the side and below smaller examples of similar figures.

The legend of the temple is one in which there is more of human interest than usually finds its way into Hindu mythology. It is said that two Brahmins of Vidyanagar, a young man and an old, went on pilgrimage together and came at last to Brindaban. There in the presence of Gopal, an incarnation of Krishna, the elder promised the younger that he would give him his daughter in marriage. But when they returned to Vidyanagar, the old man found that a husband sometimes proposes and his wife and her relations dispose. So many objections were raised to the match that the old man was driven to giving to the young Brahmin evasive replies. At last he openly denied that he had made any promise. The younger Brahmin answered angrily, in the presence of the united opponents to his marriage, that such a promise, having been made in the presence of the god, could not be broken. But they only laughed at him and told him to bring his witness.

Accordingly he returned to Brindaban and there prayed the god to go to Vidyanagar to attest the promise. Krishna consented on condition that the Brahmin would exhibit his faith by never looking back when on the road. He kept his promise until within a few miles of his destination. Then, as with Lot's wife, curiosity grew too much for him and he looked back. Thereupon the god stood firm and would not move. However, the Brahmin went on to his former companion's house and called to those inside to come to see how Krishna bore witness to a promise. They went and to their amazement saw the image of Krishna standing in the centre of the plain that surrounded the city. Confronted with this supernatural evidence the old Brahmin held to his bargain,

SAKHIGOPAL: THE BATHING TANK.

the younger married his daughter, and the King built a great temple on the spot.

The image reached its quiet resting place in the garden at Satyabadi after being taken as one of the spoils of Vidyanagar by Purushottamadeva, who, in the last years of the fifteenth century, captured the city. He installed it at Cuttack, but it was removed to Satyabadi during the Mogul Rule in Orissa.

CHAPTER XIV.

Shrine and Sea-Beach.

JAI Jagannath ki Jai!"—Hail, O Lord of the World Hail !—has been the salutation of millions of pilgrims through a thousand years and more as they have sighted from afar the dome of the great temple of Jagannath.

"Jai Jagannath ki Jai !". The shout has gone up from travel-parched throats throughout centuries; arms weary with the carrying of burdens many scores of "kos" have lifted to salute the great white dome; garments with the dust and mud of many provinces have been changed. and the puja dress put on to do honour to the god; and tired feet—many bleeding from rough ways and others wrapped in blood-stained bandages—have been set forward once more on the road that leads to the most holy shrine of the Hindus. "Jai Jagannath ki Jai !". Still that shout rings out from young and old and rich and poor as the wheel-topped tower lifts above the low horizon of trees from the pilgrimage road over the bridge of eighteen arches or from the Bara Danda, where the pilgrims who have come by train first see the temple. And with that cry upon their lips they hurry on to "pay homage to the gods with the dust on the feet."

The name of Puri is of recent bestowal. Throughout the antique literature of India, in the inscriptions to

PURI : THE GREAT TEMPLE.

be found in temples and on rocks it is only spoken of as Purushottoma, Purushottoma-kshetra or Sri-kshetra, or Purushottoma Kalatra (camp). The Mussulman historians also wrote of it in this manner, while early European writers always spoke of "the great city Juggarnat." The name of Puri or Pooree first appeared after the British conquest, in conjunction with Jagannath, the city being called Jagannath-Pooree or Jagannath's City, and at last simply Pooree. A simplification of spelling has led to the change to Puri, and the name has commended itself to the popular taste as a handy abbreviation.

For centuries the worship of Jagannath has been carried on in Puri, but not always in the great temple that now rises from within its battlemented walls of laterite. Eight hundred years ago, however, the present temple was built in the reign of Chodagangedeva, the first Eastern Ganga King of Orissa.

Since that time millions of pilgrims must have visited the city of the Lord of the World; gazed up the wide Bara Danda or Car Road along which the gods are drawn to the Garden of Pleasure to the great dome of the temple rising white above a thousand roofs; helped to haul the three great cars by the mighty ropes, thereby gaining many blessings and the remission of all sins.

The legend of the origin of Jagannath goes back to the golden age, when the King of Malwa sent out Brahmans to seek out Vishnu. One of these devotees, named Vidyapati, travelled through the jungles until he came to the country of the Savars. There he dwelt in the house of a pious fowler who was a servant of the god Jagannath, and daily offered him flowers and fruit in secret. Vidyapati won the friendship of the fowler, who showed him his god—a blue stone at the foot of a tree. And one day while these two were placing their floral offerings before the stone there came a great voice out of the jungle, saying—"O faithful servant, I am wearied of these jungle flowers and fruits, and crave for cooked rice and sweetmeats. No longer shalt thou see me in the form of thy blue god. Hereafter I shall be known as Jagannath, the Lord of the World."

Vidyapati hailed the revelations of the voice with delight and returned to the King to announce his discovery. Indradyumna marshalled his army and marched through the untravelled jungles. But at the holy spot there was no blue stone. It had disappeared the day the Brahmin left, having been caught up in a sandstorm. The King was much cast down

IN THE SURF AT PURI.

and had begun to perform penances when another voice came out of the clouds crying, that if he offered a thousand asvamedha sacrifices he would be blessed with the sight of Vishnu not in the shape of the blue image but of a log bearing certain marks. Indradyumna complied with the celestial order for sacrifices, and thereupon the god appeared in the form of a log floating on the sea. This was brought ashore and installed on the site of the enclosure in which the sacrifices had been performed. This place has been identified as the site of Jagannath's garden house at Puri.

Indradyumna then gathered together all the carpenters of the country and bade them fashion the log into an image of Jagannath. But when they put their chisels into the wood, the iron lost its edge: when they raised the mallets to strike the chisels they missed their blows and injured their own hands. Then Vishnu, in the form of an aged carpenter, appeared and offered to make the log into an image if he were left alone with it for fifteen days. Here there is a deviation of the story. According to one account, at the end of the allotted time the king found that the carpenter had disappeared and left three images, fashioned from the waist upwards, of Jagannath and his brother and sister. But Jagannath and his brother had only stumps for arms and the sister no arms at all. Another story says that the Queen insisted upon the carpenter being disturbed before the fifteen days were completed and that he accordingly left the images unfinished. With these three gods to house, Indradyumna built a temple a hundred cubits high for their reception. He then went to heaven to ask Brahma

PURI : THE WATER-BABIES.

to consecrate the images and shrine. Brahma came "in a moment," but with Brahma a moment lasts for many ages and in the meantime Indradyumna had been forgotten and another king reigned in his stead. Indradyumna's arrival rather complicated affairs but he was able to assure the new king of his peaceful purpose and the images were then brought into the temple and consecrated by Brahma.

The daily ceremonies before the gods are numerous. First comes the early morning opening of the doors of the shrines, before which a hymn is sung in order that the gods may know that the sun has risen. Their couches, upon which they are supposed to have reclined during the night, are then removed and the ceremony of lighting camphor in silver salvers and waving blazing torches before the gods is carried out. In the gloom of the innermost shrine the ceremony must be most picturesque, the lurid flames lighting up the rude gaudy images and the glistening bodies of the priests. A cake of rice flour and water is then offered and a wick placed in this is lighted and the whole waved before the gods. A gong sounds and the Joya Bejoya door is opened and the waiting multitudes outside then see the forms of the gods in the glare of the torches. Then arises the cry from the concourse of worshippers: "Take pity on me, O God, and free me from all my woe."

The gods are then bathed and dressed, all being done vicariously. The teeth are cleaned—always a highly important ritual in the Indian's life—by a rubbing of the reflection of the god's mouth in a brass dish, and water is poured into brass tubs to signify the ablutions. Then the gods are dressed, clothes being placed before them and rubbed with camphor. The early breakfast is then placed before the gods and other offerings are made, this time of money by the people. About 10 A.M. a breakfast is offered, the imaginary repast being enlivened by a girl dancing a measure to the sound of a drum.

After the mid-day meal the gods enjoy a siesta, the cots being brought in from the store-room. In the evening other meals are offered. At ten o'clock silver cups containing essence of sandal wood are brought in and the liquid is poured over the bodies of the gods. Pilgrims are then admitted again to the inner temple. At midnight the gods are garlanded ; music and singing follows ; the couches are again brought in, and the curious trinity composed to sleep,

PURI FISHERMEN.

In addition to this daily ceremonial there are sixty-two festivals in the year, arranged chiefly according to the months. The most important of all is the Rath Jatra, or Car Festival which commemorates the victorious journey of Krishna from Gokul to Mathura, and which has brought Puri and its great Jagannath cars into pre-eminence all over the civilised world. The legend of the journey in Hindu mythology is that Vishnu or Krishna was the eighth son of Vasudeva and his wife Devaki. It having been predicted that a son of theirs would kill Kansa, the demon king of Mathura, who typifies the principle of evil, Kansa imprisoned the pair and killed their six sons. Balarama, the seventh, was transferred from the womb of Devaki to that of Rohini, another wife of Vasudeva and so saved. On the night of the birth of Krishna, the father miraculously escaped from his prison and crossing the Jamuna entrusted the infant to the herdsman king of Braja. There Gopal or Krishna grew up to manhood. Then Kansa heard of him and sent a messenger to bring him and his brother to Mathura. Instead of coming submissively they drove in a war chariot to the place, slew Kansa, and Krishna reigned in his stead.

The journey is typified by the journey of Jagannath, Balabhadra and Subhadra (his brother and sister) in the Jagannath cars to the garden house along the Bara Danda Road. This great thoroughfare of the gods is a mile and a half long and eighty yards broad. Down the centre of it runs a more or less level path of red sand; on either side grass reaches to the houses and shops that crowd, in typically Indian fashion, along its borders. The procession of the gods is the great event of the year at Puri, and on this occasion (which takes place in June or July) the long wide road is black with people from all over India. Every year now-a-days the total reaches over a lakh of pilgrims and in 1912, when, according to traditional practice the images were renewed (an event occurring every thirty-six years) there were 300,000 people present. Of this number 160,000 were brought in by the Bengal Nagpur Railway. Babel is no word for the multitude of tongues that are spoken on these occasions. Almost every "bat" in Hindustan—and there are hundreds—is heard, and the most accomplished linguist cannot hope to make himself understood or to understand all the strange lingos about him.

The Jagannath cars are huge, ponderous vehicles, devoid of any beauty, and barbaric both in construction and decoration. They are supported on sixteen huge wheels, each seven feet in height and placed beneath the car in pairs. The structures are round at the base, and these huge wheels rumble along under the centre as well as at the sides. The design is ingenious but affords few facilities for steering, with the result that the great chariots pursue anything but a straight course. The cars rise in tiers until the platform upon which the god is placed is reached. The gaudiest and most barbaric decorations imaginable are used, and as the cars rumble and jolt along, they are one great blaze of colour. The car of Jagannath is the largest, being 45 feet high and 35 feet at the base. The other cars are a little smaller.

The sacred moment of the removal is when the images are brought out of the Lion Gate of the temple to be placed on the chariots. Then the assembled thousands fall prostrate, or as prostrate as the crush will allow, and bow their foreheads in the dust. This act of adoration finished, they seize the giant ropes, each as thick as a man's thigh, and pull the cars slowly with many false movements towards the Garden of Pleasure. The journey is supposed to take a few hours, but it has been known to occupy days, inasmuch as the inability to guide the cars causes them to run off the road and to sink deep into the soft sand at the sides. At the garden the images are placed in the shrine for a week and are then brought back to the temple. By this occasion, however, many of the pilgrims have departed and professional car-pullers have often to be engaged to haul the gods back to their temple.

A tradition has attained wide credence in English literature that many of the people who go to Puri for the Jagannath festival seek death under the wheels of the cars in order that they may secure certain admission to the paradise in which they believe. Bruton, the first Englishman to visit Puri and who brought to play upon the festival the cold light of a believer among heathens, was very severe upon the "abominable custom" among the pilgrims at Puri and was probably responsible for starting the belief. For in his description of the temple he wrote: "And when it (the chariot of Jagannath) is going along the city, there are many that will offer themselves a sacrifice to this idol, and desperately lie down on the ground,

PURI : THE JAGANNATH CARS.

that the chariot wheels may run over them, whereby they are killed out-right; some get broken arms, some broken legs, so that many of them are destroyed, and by this means they think to merit Heaven."

Bernier and Alexander Hamilton supported the idea, the former declaiming: "And while the chariot of hellish triumph pursues its solemn march, persons are found (it is no fiction which I recount) so blindly credulous and so full of evil notions as to throw themselves upon the ground in the way of its ponderous wheels, which pass over and crush to atoms the bodies of the wretched fanatics without exciting the horror or surprise of the spectators." In fact the supposition that the Jagannath car took its toll yearly of the flesh and blood of India has given rise to bye-words and phrases that find many a place in English writings.

It is the more satisfactory to record, then, that self-immolation was never practised by the devotees of Jagannath. Such deaths as did occur beneath the remorseless wheels of the car were for the most part due to accident, and not to any suicidal design on the part of the sufferers. A few deaths may occur among "diseased or incurable objects," as Sir William Hunter puts it, "who took this means to put themselves out of pain." The great majority of tragedies, however, were due only to the multitudes rushing forward to obtain a glimpse of the "god in the car," in which the weak and old, and especially the women, were flung down, and, unable to recover themselves, were under the wheels which, with the weight they support and their immovability, cannot be stopped or guided. Now-a-days an accident never occurs, for the greatest care is exercised in keeping back the crowds, and police are always stationed about the chariot, marching in front and at the sides in order to rescue any who fall in dangerous positions. For many years now no deaths have been recorded beneath the once fatal wheels of Jagannath.

The great temple dominates the landscape at Puri just as the great festival of Rath Jatra dominates the Hindu year. From most points of view its enormous white fluted corbel with its gigantic wheel—the emblem of Vishnu—and fluttering red flags flying out to all the winds of heaven is the centre of the picture. Raised against the clear blue sky of winter, the deeper azure of the hot weather, or the dull grey of the monsoons the tapering tower presents a spectacle of grandeur, power and romance. As one drives up the great Bara Danda the view of the temple is superb. Out of a cluster of low buildings, other spires and smaller towers, leap two great elongated domes, one a deep greyish brown and the other an almost dazzling white. Outside the grey crenulated walls, which rise almost hidden amid a host of buildings both inside and outside the temple, stand the three cars of Jagannath rude in the manufacture, barbaric in their decoration, gaudy in their colouring; typical of the faith they symbolise. They are as much the emblems of Jagannath as the majestic building they almost hide.

Standing outside the wall among the hordes of people of all *jats* and *bats* that are continually congregating at Puri, one can get some idea of the glories of the sculpture with which the whole of the building is embellished; the elaborate carvings and mouldings that are piled one upon another, wherever there is space. For Jagannath claims with the main temple at Bhubaneswar the credit of being among the finest examples of Orissan architecture.

No European is allowed inside the temple, but a fine view of the interior of the courtyard—tiers of steps rising one above another to the great entrance of the refectory hall—is obtained through the high and narrow porch doorway of the Lion Gate.

There are many other temples at Puri, but all lack interest in comparison with that of Jagannath. The garden house of the god, to which he is drawn on the occasion of the Rath Jatra, is, however, to be seen. It is a white building containing a hall and two shrines. Its garden effect has now long departed and the compound is flagged and built up with shelters for pilgrims and offices. The only reminders of a garden are pigeons fluttering on the roof of the shrine and a chital or small spotted deer that wanders about the compound.

Puri is, indeed, among the glories of India and none can claim having visited the chief of the notable places of the Empire if the city has been neglected. Not only is it one of the chief places of pilgrimage in the most prolific land of pilgrimages in the world, but it is among the artistic and architectural glories of a country peculiarly rich in such monuments of the past. The whole of the religious buildings are evidences not only of the genius of the past and of the wonderful work of a civilisation that existed while Europe was still deep in barbarism, but it is a proof of the devoticn that gave to the faith of the people the highest development of their art.

In addition to its archæological, historical, and architectural interest, Puri is a popular health resort that well deserves the reputation it has for building up energies slackened by the muggy heat of Calcutta, for restoring highly strung nerves to their normal quietness, and for bringing back strength after a bad "go" of one of the many little attacks of illness to which residents in Calcutta are subject. Puri has several advantages over the only other holiday places within easy reach of the people of Bengal's chief city. In the first place it is only a night's run and so lends itself more or less to a week-end, although a longer stay than the proverbial "Saturday to Monday" holiday is needed if the full benefits of the ocean breezes are to be obtained. Then Puri is still in the plains and that means that there is no violent change from great heat to moderate cold to be undergone, as in a trip to the hills. Many people who run up to the lower ranges of the Himalayas for a holiday are more or less upset for a week after their arrival and are still more likely to be affected on a sudden return to the moist terrors of the plâins. Such an attack very often neutralises the effect of a holiday in the hills. But Puri avoids both these drawbacks. At the same time it is distinctly cooler than Calcutta and, what is more, the air has a quality that is rare to one who knows only the humid atmosphere of the banks of the Hooghly. For (and in the third place) Puri is one of India's few sea-side places, and that means that it possesses bracing breezes, keen air, and a restorative atmosphere as well as one of the amenities of sea-side life—bathing. But the chief thing about Puri is its healthy winds that blow the listlessness out of the jaded "Ditcher" and present him with some of the feeling of vigour, which, if he has been in Calcutta for long, he knows only as a memory. So strong and regular are the winds in Puri that although it should by methods of comparison be hotter than Calcutta—it is further in the tropics—punkhas are rarely needed in the European houses on the beach, so equable and pleasantly cool is the temperature even in the hottest months of the year.

Puri has caught on with the people of Calcutta and is becoming yearly more popular. But the present accommodation for visitors is notoriously inadequate and what is really needed is a good hotel. With such an addition to its attractions Puri would rapidly increase a popularity already considerable.

The chief pleasure at Puri is, of course, the sea and sea-bathing. The effect of the sea upon the majority of human creatures is well known. Even old ladies who would never think of showing even a stockinged ankle in the ordinary way will, with well-kilted skirts, risk a paddle in an inch of water. Normal persons when they visit the sea, fly to gay, sometimes daring, bathing costumes. The fashionable miss enjoys the opportunity the beach offers for an exhibition of her charms. So it is at Puri. Every one bathes when the tide serves, and as there is no mugwump of a parish council and no Mrs. Grundy, all visitors revel happily in the surf. Many wear a sun hat of straw that gives them the appearance of soldiers in Assyrian bas-reliefs and adds greatly to the picturesqueness of the scene.

The bathing needs care and a regard for advice, as it does at all sea-side places. The undertow is

PURI : THE BATHERS.

strong and one should not venture out of depth, or the current will probably carry out the careless bather, necessitating his ignominious retrieval by a fisherman. The great scheme is to sit, or lie, on the wet sand and let the breakers dash over one, floating in the shallows until they recede. Or if you be venturesome, you may go and stand a little deeper and endure a trial of strength with old Neptune's white horses. They often prostrate you, but, if you be far enough inshore, do not carry you out to "their pastures"—which is as well for you. Many happy hours are spent on the shore at Puri, and any one who once becomes a "surf-baby" thinks ever after of his days at Puri with the smile that the happiest of recollections brings to the lips and eyes.

Yet another amusement is to watch the fishermen in their masula boats and catamarans. The former are flat-bottomed craft of planks sewed together with cane straps, and are eminently adapted for crossing the surf as they give to the waves.

Catamarans are composed of four tree trunks held together by wooden pegs, the tree trunks in the centre acting as a keel. The ease with which the fishers manage these apparently unhandy vessels and their skill in the water is one of the revelations of the foreshore.

But, perhaps, even when the attractiveness of Puri as a health resort is considered, the chief interest of the place for some minds is in the famous temple of Jagannath and in the historical and religious associations with which that picturesque edifice is connected. To the European, Puri is but a holiday station. To the Indian it is "the City of Jagannath, the Lord of the World."

CHAPTER XV.

The Black Pagoda.

In the early days of European navigation to India—and probably before that when the Indians themselves were sailors of some repute—vessels beating up the flat, sandy surf-beaten western coast of the Bay of Bengal took as landmarks at one stage two great buildings that stood almost on the sea-shore—the "White Pagoda" and the "Black Pagoda." The White Pagoda was the Jagannath Temple at Puri, the shining wheel-topped corbel of which can be seen by land and sea for many miles. The Black Pagoda was the temple of Arka, the Sun god, at Konarak, twenty odd miles north of Puri along the sea coast. But while the shrine of Jagannath still retains its prosperity, its sanctity and its attraction for hordes of pilgrims yearly—the number of devotees has largely increased with the introduction of travelling facilities—that of Arka has, like Dogberry, had misfortunes, look you. It now possesses but a shadow of its former grandeur. The greater part is ruined to such an extent that entrance to the temple is impossible; the compound is a chaos of broken laterite and marble; and its twelve great festivals in the year have dwindled to one. Yet bereft of all its glories and reduced to a mere shell amid debris, Konarak must undoubtedly be visited if one desires to claim a knowledge of the wonders of India; indeed, of the world. The temple, dilapidated as it is, is a wonderful example of the heights to which both the arts of architecture and sculpture had reached even centuries ago.

But one does not achieve the conquest of this wonderful monument of the marvels of antiquity with ease. The journey is, indeed, discouraging. Konarak lies twenty-one miles north-east of Puri town. The nearest station is Puri ; the only road lies across a waste of dunes, here and there held together with short rough grass, but mostly fine loose sand in which one sinks at every step. The only mode of covering the journey is by palki or bullock cart. The palki, borne by six men, with a relay, does the journey in seven or eight hours ; a bullock cart takes a good thirteen or fourteen. There are suggestions that one might reach Konarak by motor from Puri along the hard sand left by the receding tide, but the season of the year must be chosen ; the cold weather with its slack tides is necessary, and the time of the journey will depend upon the tides. Probably an excursion of this sort would be somewhat in the nature of an experiment.

Nevertheless there are compensations to the palki and the byle-gari. One receives new sensations, for instance. But the bullock cart is the more prolific in these. In the palki you can merely recline and listen to the laboured breathing, shuffling footsteps and ceaseless praying grunts of the coolies. You are swung along easily but with little interest in the world about you. With a bullock cart you can enter more into the spirit of the journey ; glean something of the mystery of the tropical night and the stars ; appreciate the devotion of such as make the journey to Konarak from a

KONARAK : THE PORCH OF THE SUN TEMPLE.

sense of religious duty. You leave Puri probably about six o'clock with the golden light of the setting sun casting long shadows before you. Into the Bara Danda, past the Garden of Pleasure of Jagannath and his brother and sister and out into the night through little villages, the bullocks set the slow even pace they will maintain till Konarak is reached.

After some three miles the route branches off from the already sufficiently kutcha road into the sand and you feel that you are at last launched upon the journey. If you get away from the tinkle of the bullock bells and the rustle of the wheels in the sand you can hear the whisper of the sea beating upon the shore, a mile or more distant. All around you stretches a waste of sand, light about your feet, black at the near margin. Now and again a palm, a sentinel to point the way, cuts up into the starry sky. A low hill heaves its black shoulder against the dimness ; or a patch of coarse grass makes the underfoot darker and better going. Of course you get tired of the bullock crawl--very tired. So you walk with your little caravan and you imagine you feel very like a patriarch in the wilderness.

The leading gariwallah has swung a lantern beneath his cart the better to see the road, and the light spreads across the sand till it meets the blackness of your horizon. The glow is ceaselessly cut up by the revolving spokes passing like shadows across a dial, running out to the edge of your little world. You walk in the light and watch the effect with some fascination. It passes the time for one thing and you forget how slowly you are travelling ; how your feet sink at every step ; forget, even, to wonder how many hours the journey

KONARAK : THE HORSES OF THE SOUTH GATE.

will really take. A gariwallah will sing in a high strained voice a stanza from some Ooryia ballad, or perhaps a prayer for a prosperous journey—the beginning words sound something like " Bol Hari " ; another will repeat a couple of phrases an octave lower and all will then be silent except for an occasional exclamation to the bullocks and the sound of a blow ; then to the song again. So the long night passes. One may sleep in a byle-gari —the soft road lulls one and the sigh of the wheels in the sand is strangely soothing—but mostly one prefers to be walking and, now and again, picking up bearings by the stars, talking in snatches to the gariwallah, enjoying the breeze that comes from the sea, which is never wholly silent. And two-thirds of the way there is a novelty; a river to be forded. The gariwallahs go out together with lanterns to investigate the depth, the lights glimmer in the dark waters, and the voices answering that the passage can be made seem strangely distant.

With the morning light comes the first glimpse of Konarak, a pyramid-like structure apparently on a distant rise. You are yet four miles away, but you leave the garis and put in some good walking in the cool of the dawn. And as you march due east, the sun rises behind the temple in golden radiance, sending up orange streamers that throw up the shape of the building and gleam through the surrounding trees. Sunrise behind Konarak is worth almost more than the dreary journey of the night.

The Sun Temple of Konarak was not always in the middle of a sandy waste on the shores of the eternal sea. Centuries ago a great river, the Prachi, ran down to the sea past its walls, emptying its waters in the Bay of Bengal at the dead and gone port of Che-li-ta-lo. Upon the banks of this river were many great settlements and towns and there is no doubt that the pilgrims came down to Konarak by this navigable stream. Remains of former civilisations are still to be found on the banks of this almost lost river and its temples were so numerous and full of sanctity that a special guide book was compiled to recount their glories. This was in the sixth century. But the Prachi silted up, its waters were diverted, and Konarak and its little holy river, the Chandrabhaga, became deserted. The legend of the building of the Temple is found in the palm leaf chronicles and in other sources. Samba, the handsome son of Krishna and Jamvavarti, was discovered by his father dallying with his step-mother. Krishna, therefore, cursed him and he became a leper, white, ghastly, untouchable. Samba pleaded with his father and the god allowed the punishment to be reduced by favour of Surya, the Sun god. Samba began a rigorous penance in the Maitreya woods and there at last Surya appeared to him and cured his leprosy. Samba accordingly established the worship of the Sun god on the banks of the Chandrabhaga. The present Sun Temple is the second structure to be erected on the site and the original location of the legend was transplanted from the north-west of India to enhance the sanctity of Konarak, or to gain for it popular recognition as the true place for Sun worship in India—on a northern portion of the Eastern shore where the sun is naturally seen practically earlier than in any other portion of the country.

King Narascinbadera, who ruled from 1238 to 1264, built the present temple. According to local tradition it took sixteen years to construct and, viewing its majestic proportions and its multitudious carvings, one does not feel that the figure is exaggerated. The design is truly magnificent. The main building—the porch and the tower—are placed upon sixteen great wheels, so as to represent the chariot of the sun—the design is not unlike that of the Jagannath cars of Puri. The porch faces the east and here presumably Arjuna, the charioteer of the sun, drove his stone horses, portions of which still exist. At present only the porch and the base of the tower—which resembled those of Puri and the Lingaraj Temple at Bhubaneswar—remain and these in a damaged condition. The compound of the temple was 885 feet from east to west, and 535 feet from north to south. It was surrounded by a battlemented wall seven to eight feet thick and twenty-five feet high. There were three entrances to the compound with its multitude of smaller temples and other holy buildings. That on the East is the principal and is made up a flight of steps guarded by lions that have overcome elephants, which are crushing men. That on the North was through a pair of elephants trampling demons; that on the South past horses rearing over prostrate enemies. The hall on the east (which may have been a temple) is now roofless, but the four massive carved pillars and many pilasters that supported a ceiling still remain to prove the wonders of the art of the period. The porch is approached through rows of prancing horses by steps nine feet in width and rising to the

KONARAK : THE ELEPHANTS OF THE NORTH GATE.

doorway which stands on a basement sixteen feet high. It had four doors, that on the west leading to the tower, where the presiding deity was installed. The others were reached by flights of steps like those on the East. The porch walls rise for 66 feet and then incline pyramidically inwards at a graceful angle to make a ribbed dome resting on crouching lions, with a bell over it and after that a second dome. The vase-shaped finial at the top has disappeared. The whole of the exterior is absolutely covered by carvings, many nearly as large as life and of an obscene character. Others, smaller ones of the same type, are empanelled in the walls. The cornices are covered with bassi-rilievi of processions, hunting and battle scenes, occupations and amusements. A remarkable feature about many of these carvings is, as Sir William Hunter points out, that they " bear witness to an age when Hindu artists worked from nature. The nymphs are beautifully shaped women, in luscious attitudes ; the elephants move along at the elephant trot, and kneel down in the stone exactly as they did in life. Some of the latter have, however, the exaggerated ear and conventional mouth of modern Hindu sculpture and the lions must have been altogether evolved from the artists' inner consciousness. Among the life-sized pieces elephants crouch in terror under rampant lions, while mutilated human figures lie crushed beneath the flat pulpy feet of the elephants. Clubmen, griffins, warriors on prancing horses, colossal figures of grotesque and varied shape, stand about in silent staring groups. The elephants have the flabby under-lips of nature and exhibit an uniformity in all the essential points of their anatomy, with a variety in posture and detail which Hindu art has long forgotten."

The amazing thing about the Sun Temple is the extraordinary magnificent scale of the whole structure; the enormous masses of rock that were placed in position without any mechanical aid; the minute carving that covered every inch of the exterior surface. The industry and ingenuity of the builders was enormous. In one respect, however, they have been proved frauds. Their gigantic iron beams, the construction of which by the smiths of six centuries ago with their primitive forges was long a mystery, have been revealed as amazing frauds. They were formed of small lengths of iron of about a foot to one and-a-half feet in length and three to four inches square, placed end on end and side by side, as bricks are laid, and then bound together with molten iron passed round the four sides of the girder. Several of these girders lie about the compound and their fractured surfaces show the method of construction. Yet the builders must have credit for moving great blocks of stone, and one example of the work done in this direction is provided by a huge piece of sculpture that lies among the debris. It represents the lion rampant upon an elephant which projects from the front of all Orissan temple spires. The height to the top of the lion's head measures 20 feet; the base is 15 feet long and 4 feet 7 inches broad. This colossal figure was cut from two pieces of stone and both had to be raised 150 feet from the ground before they could be placed in position! Moreover the building material was brought from enormous distances. There are no stone quarries within twenty-five miles and no steatite slabs like those used in sculpture in the temple within eighty miles. Even if the building materials were carried by sea, their moving and manœuvring into position were remarkable feats.

The great disaster which robbed the Sun Temple of its tower befel in the last century, but the structure had been falling to decay long before that. Probably the difficulties of reaching Konarak after the silting up of the Prachi reduced the revenues of the edifice and repairs were neglected. Probably the domination of Moslem rule oppressed the place still more. There is a legend that the desertion of the fane was due to an extraordinary cause. It is said that a lodestone of immense size which was inserted in the tower, drew ashore (like Sindbad's rock) all vessels passing near the coast. At last under Moghul rule the crew of a passing vessel landed, attacked the temple and carried off the lodestone. The priests, alarmed at the violation of the shrine, carried the image of Surja to Puri and the temple was then deserted. But the true facts are that in 1627 the tower was so dilapidated that Raja Narasinhadeva, of Khurda, removed the image of the Sun god to the temple of Indra in the enclosure of the Jagannath temple at Puri, while the black pillar in front of the Eastern doorway was taken down and set up in front of the Lion Gate at Puri.

The reasons given for the fall of the tower are interesting. The catastrophe is ascribed by some to earthquake or lightning; by others to the failure of the foundations to sustain the enormous weight; and by other some to faulty construction. Mr. M. H. Arnott, Superintending Engineer, favours the last view. He

KONARAK : THE EASTERN GATE.

explains that the temple was built over a core of sand upon which the stones were ramped, and the sand removed by the four doors. The system upon which the towers in Orissan architecture were built is that by which the final melon-shaped dome or "amla" locks all the stones of the corbelled walls together, much as does the keystone of an arch. Its weight tends to crush the tower stones but its pressure keeps them in. The construction at Konarak being faulty, the removal of the support given by the sand at last caused the weight of the amla to counterbalance its pressure power and the corbelling walls were forced inwards. It may be also that on the decrease in revenues, trees and plants were allowed to grow on the tower and these loosened the dome and the topmost stone slab, which then fell during one of the strong south-easterly gales that lash the coast of the Bay. The remaining stones followed in due course, probably at infrequent intervals.

After the desertion of the shrine it was almost buried by blown sand and for many years but little of the temple was visible. In 1902 however, Government directed that the conservation of the edifice should be undertaken and the efforts of the Archæological Survey have resulted in a great change for the better. The great courtyard has been excavated; the whole of the gateways with their elephants, horses, and lions exposed to view, and flights of steps to the doors of the porch uncovered; the basement with its sixteen chariot wheels unearthed; doorways and dangerous quarters repaired and the porch filled with stone and sand to prevent its following the example of the tower; carvings ranged in order; the sanctum with its exquisitely carved steatite throne for the image, cleared of the debris of the tower; and casuarina trees planted to prevent the sand drifting again upon the temple.

Such is the sun temple of Konarak to-day, worthy indeed of all trials and difficulties of the journey. Its grandeur is, indeed, unsurpassed even in its present state and one may well quote Mr. Marshall, Director-General of Archæology, when he says: "There is no monument of Hinduism, I think, that is at once so stupendous and so perfectly proportioned as the Black Pagoda, and none which leaves so deep an impression on the memory. When Ferguson wrote of it so admiringly, he had seen but half its beauty. The deep and richly carved basement with the horses and chariots of the Sun god had not been unearthed in his day, nor were any traces visible of the massive dancing hall in front, which makes such a splendid addition to the main buildings."

Truly the sightseer who misses the Black Pagoda is passing by one of the most amazing of the relics of India of the past.

CHAPTER XVI.

The Temple of Eleven Hundred Steps.

IT is at once an obvious remark and a platitude to say that the beautiful and the rare are always difficult of attainment. But most people think in platitudes and convert them into obvious remarks. And so one may be forgiven for the obviousness of all the above and perhaps permitted to add that many quotations concerning the platitudinous and wise saws regarding the obstacles in the way of achieving high ambitions occurred to the mind on the road to and from the temple at Simhachalam. For in addition to a bullock-cart ride of three miles (as the local people say) though truth bids one to admit that it seems more like five, the temple is only reached by the climbing of eleven hundred steps—eleven hundred and twenty to be precise. After all the " byle-gari " ride was not so uncomfortable. The road was excellent, the bullocks trotted willingly nearly all the way, and the gari-walla had put a new palmyra mat on the floor and a new interior thatching of the same useful material, so that the cart smelt as sweet as new-mown hay and one was strongly tempted to make off with the mat as a specimen of neat and clever workmanship. The Telegu who drove was more merciful to his beast than he at Bhubaneswar ; also the bullocks were in fine condition and showed no marks of ill usage.

The road wound around the ghauts through patches of jungle and past cultivated lands and countless palmyra trees standing sentinel along its course until it reached the little village of Simhachalam, which is much more famous than it looks at the first blush. For the place is as noted for oranges and pine-apples as Alamanda, a few stations away, is for mangoes and Ichchhapuram in Ganjam for plantains. Above all the village produces glorious roses and in the cold weather the show in the rose-garden attached to the Maharaja of Vizianagram's Rest House—open also to Europeans—is one of the sights of the place.

SIMHACHALAM : A TEMPLE MUSICIAN.

But above all these, the place is known for its temple of Varahanarasimhaswamy, perched high on the side of the hill that overshadows the village. Approaching the place the rider in the bullock cart sees high up, among the luxuriant foliage that fringes the steep ascent, a little white temple ; further up he catches a shadowy glimpse of yet other buildings. He also sees, climbing the hill, a steep series of steps. A nearer sight of these is a "staggerer." From the entrance they arise in an unbroken line as far as

SIMHACHALAM : HALF WAY UP THE ELEVEN HUNDRED STEPS.

the eye can see for the over-hanging trees. But even in this view the half is not nearly told. However, he who "maun to Cupar, maun to Cupar" and one essays to climb the heights. The steps take you gently at first, up little flights—five or six—and long landing spaces of two or three yards. But the higher the climber goes the longer becomes the flights until eleven is the average. Sometimes one does thirteen with a struggle, pauses for breath, and wonders why it was necessary to build a famous shrine in the sky. After some ten minutes mountaineering one rounds a corner and comes in view of the temple entrance—dark, forbidding, cavernous, and standing at the head of a still longer flight than any yet encountered. Here the weary may look back and see and admire, amid the trees, the fertile plains below stretched out like a map. Then, again, towards the crest. The interior of the temple is a garden, full of little cascades, carved wells, great trees, and overhanging rocks. Through these the stairway winds in spasms of thirty and forty steps at a time. The last section is, however, easier going and the garden is more picturesque. Then, through two white gateways into a little village, where no cart has ever come or ever will come and finally round a bend, the shrine—white towers against the verdure and grey rocks of the hill—leaps into view. There are still more steps to the entrance and many carvings, but to the visitor the chief attraction of the visit will probably be that he has climbed a bigger staircase than most of his acquaintances.

The temple is five hundred years old and the stairway a hundred and fifty. The latter was built by a

Maharaja of Vizianagram, so said the calmly-spoken Superintendent, and the building was distinctly a pious and thoughtful act, as the ascent of the rocky hill without such an aid must have been a journey of considerable fatigue and trouble. Two great festivals take place in the year, and the general annual attendance at the temple numbers about twenty thousand, mostly Telegus.

And so to the bottom again, taking some care that one does not take the whole eleven hundred in one glorified glissade.

CHAPTER XVII.

Vizag., Waltair and their Past.

WALTAIR and Vizagapatam—" Vizag." for short—are places of which the Bengal Nagpur Railway Company has great hopes in the future development of their line. They lie on the sea coast within a mile and a half of each other, and it is the intention if possible to make Waltair as successful and popular a holiday resort as Puri, and Vizag. one of the great ports of India. Both have enormous possibilities in these directions.

Waltair is already very well known and liked by residents of Madras and a few of Calcutta who wish to exchange the heat of those cities for a breath of cooler air. It has a sloping beach upon which the restless surf beats with ceaseless moaning roar, and here and there clusters of rocks fling the breaking waves high into a tower of spray. At the southern end of the beach rises the steep promontory of the Dolphin's Nose—and few capes have been more aptly named. Behind the sandy beach the ground climbs to a great height and upon this ridge many European bungalows have been built, each in its own compound of rock gardens and in a position to receive the full benefits of the cool breezes from the Bay of Bengal. Indeed, so bracing are these winds that Waltair has been called the " Brighton of India." Such fame it

WALTAIR : THE COIR ROPE MAKERS.

WALTAIR: THE ROMAN CATHOLIC CHURCH.

may hardly yet merit, but there is no reason to doubt that in the future it will approach nearly in popularity and health-giving usefulness to the English "Queen of Watering-places".

Apart from its picturesque situation Waltair is notable for being the head-quarters of a Roman Catholic Bishopric; and a great Catholic School, a Convent, and a fine Church perched high upon the dizzy slope of a hill bear testimony to the zeal and organising powers of the clergy in the neighbourhood. The Roman Catholic Church stands on the same hill and slightly higher than a Hindu Temple and a Moslem Mosque and it is said that a similar collection of beliefs in so limited an area is unknown in any other part of the world.

Waltair is a popular little place and contains many amenities of a European station such as a Club, a Hotel and a Dak Bungalow. On its beach may be seen many quaint little scenes; women beating coir out of cocoanuts to make ropes and the fishermen completing the ropes for their boats; many others making their nets; divers old men and chòkras digging in the soft sand for crabs after tickling them with a long spear of grass to make sure that they are at home in their holes; and a fleet of fishing boats tossing and tumbling on the blue waters of the Bay.

Vizagapatam, at one time of great importance whe the British held it as a stronghold of the Coromandel Coast after dispossessing the Dutch, promises to surpass its old glories if the scheme for the formation of a harbour in the backwater behind the Dolphin's Nose comes

WALTAIR: THE CRABCATCHER.

WALTAIR: THE DOLPHIN'S NOSE.

WALTAIR: SURF ON THE BEACH.

into being. The importance of the scheme can be seen at once if a map of India is placed open besides the reader. There are, south of the Bengal Nagpur line from Howrah to Nagpur, no lines connecting the Central Provinces with the coast and indeed no connection with Southern India between Howrah and Bezwada and Bombay and Hotgi. Thus all the produce of the Central Provinces must be railed east and west for export. Continual delays occur as the result of this system and the Central Provinces authorities are pressing for the continuation of a line from Raipur to Vizianagram and thence along the existing route to Vizag. which will allow their produce reaching the sea with less delay and at cheaper rates. The Bengal Nagpur Railway on their part are urging the construction of a harbour in the great backwater that lies behind Vizag. The extent of the land-locked water is several miles and after being dredged it would make an ideal harbour. The narrow entrance is off the shore at Waltair beneath the shelter of the huge promontory

VIZAGAPATAM : THE PROPOSED HARBOUR.

of the Dolphin's Nose and its length is only a quarter of a mile. Indeed it is claimed that Vizag. could have one of the best and safest harbours in the world if the scheme were brought into being. The matter is now before the Government of India, the Central Provinces Government, and the Board of the Railway Company.

CHAPTER XVIII.

An Indian Pilgrimage.

INDIA is a land of pilgrimages. Throughout the length and breadth of the vast tracts of country in which Hinduism is the predominating faith, parties are always coming and going upon journeys to the shrines of one or other of the enormous conglomeration of gods and goddesses, which, by their cross-referenced names, make Hindu mythology so puzzling to the general reader. There are scores of places of pilgrimage scattered over the country—Benares, Brindaban, Puri, Kalighat, Bhubaneswar, for instance, all claim their thousands of devotees yearly. At some seasons villages are almost deserted in order that the population may ensure themselves blessings in this world and happiness, or at least a reduction of misfortunes, in the many others in which a Hindu believes.

Kalighat, a temple situated in Calcutta, during the Kali and Durga Pujas (in September or October), is literally besieged by thousands of people from all parts of Bengal, where the Mother and the Goddess of Destruction—Kali is both—is peculiarly venerated. Little crowds of devotees pick their way along the busy streets of Calcutta and across the green maidan, many walking painfully, almost crawling through fatigue; others going cheerily upon their way with laugh and jest; divers more—especially old women—carrying

KALIGHAT : KALI'S TEMPLE.

huge bundles on their heads, as well as lotas and other utensils, and little idols and keepsakes of their journey in their hands. They pass by in strings, hundreds upon hundreds, jostling along with a hardly perceptible patter of bare feet, a little laughter, and occasionally a full-throated quavering song to keep them company on their way. All bear upon their foreheads the red mark of the pilgrim who has achieved his desire, all are garlanded with red and yellow flowers; all bear the trials of travel patiently and with good heart.

Some trials, of course, there must be; some little tribulations that those unused to long journeys cannot avoid. But to-day the difficulties are as nothing to what they were in the past. The railways have robbed these journeys of nine-tenths of their terrors and a pilgrimage in India to-day, as in other parts of the world, has lost its old meaning of hardships and fatigue, and sometimes of tragedy, and partakes more of the nature of a holiday. As a matter of fact, it is so regarded by many of the people. The Pujas and the Raths of India are to-day among the social festivals and many a villager puts by his savings to spend upon a trip to a shrine in much the same spirit as the Manchester cotton worker saves up for his Whitsuntide burst at Blackpool. Not only do thousands of pilgrims visit temples and shrines, but they take full advantage of the opportunity to "see the sights" as well. In Calcutta the Zoological Gardens and the Indian Museum are as much to be inspected as Kalighat is to be visited, and hundreds of men, women and children wander round-eyed and open-mouthed among these wonders.

At Puri the Bengal Nagpur Railway pays particular attention to the needs and comforts of the lakhs of pilgrims who annually traverse huge distances to worship the Lord of the World. They are attended to in every possible manner; every want supplied; every danger decreased to vanishing point; every suffering relieved; and in fact they are almost, as an old lady would say, "cosseted."

To those who knew the pilgrimage of old before the railways stepped in to make the way smooth for the devotee the change is remarkable. In former times a pilgrimage was, indeed, a venture upon which the most hardy might look with some fear. It meant, perhaps, a march of hundreds of miles along bad, rough, stony or muddy roads ; many stoppages by the road-side ; innumerable camps beneath the stars ; dangers, sometimes death, from robbers ; certain death to many from wild animals ; certain death to others from the great epidemics that followed upon the congregation of vast crowds of human beings in restricted spaces without sanitation, without a proper water supply, and without, perhaps, a sufficiency of food. Or the pilgrim might travel for days cramped up in country boats, a prey to wind and weather, and always running the risk of fell diseases. They might voyage by sea, as they used to go to Puri ; and the Puri beach with its continuous surf only to be passed in tiny crafts is no fit place for the landing of weak women and children, or even of men unaccustomed to the perils of the great waters. Not many years ago a pilgrim ship was lost off the coast at Puri with all hands and two thousand devotees, and if a tragedy of such magnitude was unfamiliar, many deaths must have occurred in the waves that break on the sandy reaches within sight of the great temple.

Here is a picture from the pen of Sir William Hunter of the perils of such a journey fifty years ago :—

" The great spiritual army marched its hundreds, and sometimes its thousands, of miles along burning roads, across unbridged rivers, and through pestilent regions of jungle and swamps. Those who kept to the road had spent their strength long before the holy city was reached. The sturdy women of Hindustan braved it out and sang songs till they dropped, but weaker females of Bengal limped piteously along with

MEIMENSINGH MEMORIAL, KALIGHAT.

bleeding feet in silence, broken only by deep sighs and an occasional sob. Many a sickly girl died upon the road; and by the time they reached Puri, the whole party had their feet bound up in rags, plastered with dirt and blood."

Such were the terrors and perils of the past. The present, thanks to a wise policy on the part of the Bengal Nagpur Railway, is very different.

In practically all cases now the journey is made in trains in commodious carriages, at a speed that is literally incomparable with that of the past and with a minimum of inconvenience. But it is in despatching the pilgrims on their return that the Company's organization is exceptionally good. A big staff goes down to Puri to make special arrangements for the Rath Jatra, and a series of schemes has been evolved for the comfort and the safety of the thousands who make the journey.

Much difficulty was experienced at one time in booking the pilgrims. Nowadays a perfectly simple system has been introduced. It is only the giving of certain colours for different routes: white for all Bengal Nagpur Stations; red for all places reached from Howrah; green for all other destinations. The people are told to book by the colours and all difficulties have disappeared. To avoid over-crowding another ingenious series of ideas has been worked out. Four roofed enclosures have been erected, in each of which fifteen hundred people can be placed; but never more than a thousand are admitted to any one of these at any time. The pilgrims are sorted into these "pens" according to the stations for which they have booked. Specials are standing ready in the commodious station at Puri—some wait for days before going—and when a train load for one destination has collected the people are despatched in driblets to the platform. Three officials stand with ropes to divide off the people in the sheds, and only a hundred or so are let go at once. As they leave the enclosure, they are told to go quietly, that there is plenty of time, and plenty of room for all. On the platform a double line of police and coolies link hands across the space between the permanent ways, leaving two or three carriages to be occupied. These are filled first and then the coolies and police are moved up and a hundred or so more pilgrims are admitted to the platform. So the work goes on, and when the train is filled it starts. Great care is taken with the people and

PURI : "PANI" FOR THE PILGRIMS.

great sympathy is shown for their little idiosyncrasies. Thus, for instance, when a party comes from one village they try to keep together all the time. This is always permitted. Moreover, especial care is taken of the old women who are often very frail and who invariably, as is their manner the world over, carry bundles that further hamper their movements. These aged dames are helped in all possible ways and are never hurried.

Every attempt is made to secure comfort. A licensed sweetmeat vendor whose goods are inspected often and at unexpected moments travels by the train and is encouraged to sell his goods. Special carriers supply the pilgrims in the carriages with water and in no case is a lota allowed to be dipped into the bucket.

The water is ladled out of the bucket—taps are on the platform—into the people's own vessels, and thus the danger of infection of any disease that may be about to break out is minimised. Cholera, often a source of hundreds of deaths, has been almost entirely eliminated by these means. Altogether the present system of managing the pilgrim traffic on the Bengal Nagpur Railway has reached a high state of efficiency and the visitors, instead of suffering great miseries and dangers, now enjoy a holiday jaunt, from which worry and fatigue and the fear of sickness have been entirely removed.

CHAPTER XIX.

By Cow-catcher and Trolley.

THERE are more ways than one of travelling on a railway, but they do not come the way of all. It must have been a desire of every boy and indeed of many a man to ride in the cab of an engine, not to speak of a journey upon the cow-catcher, while, for some, even the slow hand-pushed trolley has a certain fascination. And in this world, when anticipation is so often the better part of a thing, it is a consolation to find that these boyish ideals of the joy-rides to be obtained on engines and trolleys are not entirely incapable of fulfilment.

When you clamber to the foot-plate and survey the world from a proud height not only physically but mentally—for you tell yourself that it is only privileged persons who can enjoy the experience you are about to undergo—the feeling is somewhat akin to that of mounting a seventeen-hands horse—at least that is what suggests itself. One is so high up in the world that things seem dwarfed, but the size of the locomotive itself—an elephantine monster from the ground—decreases perceptibly. The next impression is the change of the field of vision. One is used to a side view from a train; up here in the cab one gets a sight of the line from a new angle and along the great black shiny flank of the "iron horse." One is surprised

GARDEN REACH : THE HEAD OFFICES OF THE BENGAL NAGPUR RAILWAY.

A PERMANENT-WAY GANG AT WORK.

somewhat at both the extent and smallness of the country taken in; the long stretch of open line with the converging rails waiting to be pinched off into nothingness where the perspective takes final effect and the extraordinary reduction round curves in cuttings or jungle. What with the smoke-stack and the shoulder of the engine the view from the outer side of the curve is as limited as that on the inner. And one no longer wonders why, at times, there is so much whistling from the engine. The driver is but giving a warning to trolleymen and permanent-way repairers of his presence, for it is astonishing how quietly a train may steal up when a cutting softens the sound of the reverberating snorts of the locomotive and deadens the roar of the wheels. On a down-grade, with steam shut off, a heavy train will slip along with comparatively no sound whatever to those on the line ahead. Hence the warning note when a sharp curve is at hand.

But perhaps the most startling revelation is the strenuous life of the stoker. He adds fuel to the roaring leaping yellow flames with their background of glowing red embers on the average once every two minutes. Open swings the door of the fire box and a great heat scorches the body and limbs of those on the foot-plate. A ruddy light gleams in the dark corners of the cab. The heat seems to glance and flicker about one as the flames dance within their bright prison. But the fireman, regardless of the tremendous heat, of the glare that seems to sear the eye-balls, of the scorching wind that dries up the throat, is flinging in shovelfuls of coal, sprinkling them to right and left, distributing them evenly over the surface of the fire. His last shovelful is bestowed with a neat turn of the wrist as the shovel rests on the edge of the furnace-opening that flings a last layer in all directions. Clang! The heat and the glare are cut off as if by a magic, and the fireman goes to the side of the cab for a breath of fresh air; but in sixty seconds he is back again. Clang! Again that spectacle of ravening flames awaiting food, that terrible scorching, that ghastly glare; again the speedy spade-work; again the grateful relief. So the fireman gets through his spell, and if ever a man earned his pay it is surely be. Behind him a khalassi is shovelling coal down from the tender, breaking up the food for the giant's searing maw; sweeping up and keeping

THE CALCUTTA-BOMBAY MAIL LEAVING DAREKASA TUNNEL.

everything ship-shape. The driver, his eyes on the line, his hand within easy reach of the whistle cord, is a busy man, but his business is more that of the brain and the eye than of the hand. The general impression of life on the foot-plate is that it is one of the most strenuous modern conditions have yet produced.

But travelling in the cab must give place so far as new sensations go to riding on the cow-catcher. Here you are as a pioneer; the first explorer in a new country; the advance guard of many things. Seated on the steel platform beside the couplings you have the warmth of the engine at your back, but the wind of your passage chills you through. The actual riding is comfortable enough barring a crampy feeling where your knees touch the edges of steel and a desire to stretch your legs and lean back that needs to be kept in hand. But you forget these little disabilities in the oy of a new movement; in the whistle of the air about your ears; in the thunder of the ordered power behind. Far ahead of you stretches the steel road, two shining bars that gleam and glitter. And as fast as your speed eats them up new distances are unrolling, just as a great carpet might be flung out by the skilful hand of a giant shopman. The scenery flits by like a cinematograph picture; new vistas open out in front; the sleepers rise up to strike you, but they are always too late. Here the train is clearing miles of ghats and the atmosphere is undergoing curious changes of temperature. Deep in the cuttings the air is damp and cool—almost shrewd; out in the open the normal heat returns, tempered by the rush of air. Round the curves the whistle shrieks in your ear; on the down grade you can enjoy the smooth travelling as the great load of steel and wood and human life slips along under its own momentum; climbing, the engine pulsates, throbs, bounds under the impulse of the drive and clatter of the piston rods. Darkness is drawing in and the signal lights begin to glimmer amid the gloom of the forest. The air grows colder and in the jungles it nips you through until you long for warmer clothing and warmer air. The night mists are creeping up; shadows are falling across the line; a cheeky jackal refuses to move, despite the deep-throated blast of the whistle, until the train is thirty yards from him and then he bounds up the cutting; the sky darkens and the glow of the sunset deepens. The rush of the air is driving tears from your eyes and demands the application of your handkerchief; the great locomotive is thrusting itself along with a thunderous roar and over the great black

A PERMANENT-WAY GANG.

shoulder of the engine the evening star gleams in a dying field of saffron.

After a journey in a cow-catcher a trolley-ride would seem slow by comparison. But there are such things as motor-trollies and a motor-trolley is a distinct sensation. It is a motor chassis on four small railway wheels but with no steering gear. But what it lacks in appearance it makes up in speed, vibration, and clatter, and the man who said that when you had finished you would not be able to hear any one speak was not exaggerating. The most curious thing about a motor-trolley is that your feet are nearly touching the track, and the result is that sleepers and ballast seem to be preparing for a combined attack upon your legs which they are always too late to deliver. Every sleeper, every stone, raises itself to strike, but slips away, indistinguishable in the mist of speed. Over bridges, the gaunt black sleepers jump up singly one after the other, only to be merged into a mass as they surge beneath you. Conversation is impossible. A shouted remark, directed by a curved hand to your ear, comes faintly as a lengthy hail; your own voice in reply sounds like a wheezy time-expired gramophone doing its utmost with a worn-out needle on a cracked, uneven record. And all the time the hot air is dashing by at thirty miles an hour, you are swaying from side to side as the trolley responds to her driving power and the rattle of the wheels on the rails and the rattle of the engine combine in one hoarse roar.

After this a push trolley is a simple affair. And yet it has its points. For one thing conversation is possible. One might debate the Baconian theory, or discourse on philosophy without distraction while the trolley slips along the line. And yet the trolley is wonderful—or at least its coolies are. To most of us walking on the metals would be a feat of balancing that would entitle us to appear as a turn on the "halls." We should achieve it only by much swaying and beating of the air with the hands. But the trolley-men in India not only progress along the lines, but they run; one foot over the other, and they never put a foot wrong. Moreover, they cut along at an amazing rate, running with the body well forward and the long stride that tells of the athlete. And when they have the trolley going well they swing up to the platform and sit on the handle-bar with which they have been pushing; only to drop unerringly back again, feet in the correct position on the line, when the speed shows signs of slackening.

BY TROLLEY : THE COOLIES TAKE AN "EASY."

HOWRAH STATION : THE CALCUTTA TERMINUS OF THE BENGAL NAGPUR RAILWAY.

You may learn many things on a trolley and one is how the train-wheels make their song; how they form themselves into a melody and beat it out for half an hour or more before suddenly changing to a new rhythm. It is because of "creep," that movement of the rails forward which has always to be taken into account. Metals, when put down, are laid "square"; that is each pair is placed with the ends exactly level. In course of time the ends will be found to be three or four inches or perhaps as much as three or four feet apart; more in some cases. This is the result of "creep"; of the movement of the rails along themselves as one might say. And the curious thing is that the same pair of rails will creep in opposite directions—an occurrence usually found on curves. This development is corrected by leaving space between the metals and eventually by taking out a piece. But it is evident now how "creep" makes the song of the train for the distribution of the ends of the metals over a space of a yard or so affords each wheel a chance to make a distinct sound in passing from one rail to another. According as the interval is long or short, so the song will be made and you may hear many a favourite air played repeatedly as you loll comfortably in your bunk. And then, when the extent of the "creep" has changed, comes a new song adapted to the fresh conditions. It was worth while travelling on a trolley to learn that.

Printed by E. G. Pearson at The Times Press, Bombay, and published by R. D. Connell at the Traffic Manager's Office, Bengal Nagpur Railway House, Calcutta—3283'16